More Raves for 3:10 to BOCA

"You should buy mine son's book, you should read, and you should enjoy. If not, you should have problems."

—Mrs. Sadie Greyberg, Delray Beach, FL

"Saddle up, all you kosher cowboys and borscht-belt bucka-roos, for the funniest book since *Crime and Punishment!*"

—*Publisher's Weakly*

"I'm shocked, shocked to find that gambling is going on in here!"

—Captain Renault

"Go ahead and laugh now, but one day you, too, will be driving a big Cadillac and eating dinner at two in the afternoon."

—Mr. Morris Bender, Century Village, Pembroke Pines, FL

"For God's sake, stop quoting me already."

—Bartlett

3:10 to BOCA

✡ ✦ AND OTHER ✦ ✡
MESHUGEH TALES OF THE YIDDISH WEST

Zane Greyberg

CITADEL PRESS
Kensington Publishing Corp.
www.kensingtonbooks.com

CITADEL PRESS BOOKS are published by

Kensington Publishing Corp.
119 West 40th Street
New York, NY 10018

All Kensington titles, imprints, and distributed lines are available at special quantity discounts for bulk purchases for sales promotions, premiums, fund-raising, educational, or institutional use. Special book excerpts or customized printings can also be created to fit specific needs. For details, write or phone the office of the Kensington special sales manager: Kensington Publishing Corp., 119 West 40th Street, New York, NY 10018, attn: Special Sales Department; phone 1-800-221-2647.

CITADEL PRESS and the Citadel logo are Reg. U.S. Pat. & TM Off.

First printing: October 2009

10 9 8 7 6 5 4 3 2 1

Printed in the United States of America

Library of Congress Control Number: 2009930444

ISBN-13: 978-0-8065-3067-3
ISBN-10: 0-8065-3067-7

Contents

"Before eating, always take time to thank the food."

—Arapaho proverb

"Don't talk with your mouth full or make noise when you bend."

—Mishagossi proverb

"What is life? It is the flash of a firefly in the night. It is the breath of a buffalo in the wintertime. It is the little shadow which runs across the grass and loses itself in the sunset."

—Blackfoot proverb

"When the white man discovered this country, Indians were running it. No taxes, no debt, women did all the work. White man thought he could improve on a system like this."

—Cherokee proverb

"If there is no self, whose arthritis is this?"

—Never Buys Retail, Chief of the Grossinga tribe

"The spirits do not speak. The spirits do not blame. The spirits do not take sides. The spirits have no expectations. The spirits demand nothing of others. The spirits are not Jewish."

—Rabbi Bobby Lee Levinsky, Temple Bet Midler, Tuscaloosa, Alabama

3:10 to BOCA

Gunshmuck

Marshal Matt Dill stared across the scrub-covered plains that reached to the distant foothills.

"De vest—it is so big," he exclaimed, fingering the large silk garment he'd bought in Franklin, Missouri, just a week before. "Fortunately, dere will be a tailor in Nudge City to take it in a little." He spurred his horse Radish to the north. "After all, a new marshal must not look like a Bar Mitzvah boy, fearful and too small for his *tallis*."

Nudge City, population 83, sat on a short spur of the Santa Fe Trail, the dusty road that opened in 1821 and rolled west from Franklin to Santa Fe, New Mexico. Nudge City was established by Jewish pioneers two score years later because they wanted to stop schlepping.

"We've spent enough time wandering in deserts," founder Avram Nudge said as he emptied dirt from the communal *etrog* box.

It wasn't much of a settlement then, and it wasn't much

better in 1867. The major export was ox dung, which the Yeshiva boys collected on the trail, gave to the bubbes to boil, and shipped east as fertilizer.

"It is against the nature of a Jew to give anyone *drek*," Avram was fond of saying. "So we sell it to them."

But where there is *drek*, can a *tuchas* be far away? With prosperity came crime in the form of the Fryers' Club. This group of cut-rate cutthroats intercepted wagon trains, fed the oxen a constipating mixture of bananas and matzo, and sold inferior, cheaper chickenshit from their ranch to unwary consumers back East.

That was why aged Avram had telegraphed Washington for help. He was dead by the time help arrived, for Washington was slow to help Jews unless oil was involved. Fortunately, the town survived—if just barely.

Matt Dill was a man with deep peacekeeping experience. Though this was his first federal assignment, the thirty-year-old was a veteran of Sisterhood Bingo Night in Brooklyn and sale days at Gimbels. He was ready for anything,

"Except having to buy dis outfit retail, and without alterations," he complained as he rode into Nudge.

It was Sunday morning and the streets were thick with Jews, just like Borough Park but with the smell of drying dung.

"Which is not as bad as some Hasids," he remarked as he headed toward the center of Omain Street.

The marshal stopped in front of the storefront that said

U.S. Marshal. He dismounted, threw his reins around the hitching post, and let Radish drink from the trough. He did not know this was the town *mikvah* until he heard the rabbi yelling at the horse. Radish immediately stopped drinking for, as an Arabian, he happened to know some Hebrew.

Dill went inside. "Nu?" he said to the man behind the desk.

"Yeah, I'm Acting Deputy Nu," the Chinese gentleman replied.

The marshal introduced himself and the deputy frowned. "That vest is too big," he said.

"Tell me about it."

"My brother runs a cleaning service—I'll take care of it."

"Do I get a discount?" Dill asked.

"Does the Dowager Empress eat lo mein?"

Dill had no idea, but he laughed like he did whenever the rebbe said something that made absolutely no sense such as, "*Ale tseyn zoln bay im aroysfaln, not eyner zol im blaybn oyf tsonveytung*," which meant, "All his teeth should fall out except one to make him suffer." Still, Dill liked the deputy and was sorry to be losing him. But someone had to keep the peace . . . and someone had to deliver takeout for his wife's booming restaurant business.

After showing Marshal Dill around, Nu took the vest and stopped, silhouetted in the doorway.

"This place is lousy," he said over his shoulder.

"I'm here to make it better," Dill replied.

"No," Nu said. "I mean there are lice. Don't go in the prison cell."

The deputy left and the lawman picked up the six-pointed tin star Nu had left on the desk. He pinned it to the lapel of his dark gray *bekeshe*. The traditional garment was cut off just above the hip so he could reach his gun in a flash. The firearm was a Shalom-maker with a four-inch barrel. It used to be five inches, but he had the tip shortened, so it would weigh less and be easier to draw.

Striding into the brilliant sunlight, the marshal was nearly knocked over as the flame-haired Miss Kitsel, the saloon keeper, rushed past.

"Vere's de fire?" the marshal asked.

"At my saloon, the Dungbranch!" she shouted as she hurried ahead, trailed by the fire brigade.

Dill followed the steam-powered fire engine to an alley where twin plumes of black smoke were churning upward. They looked like the *payees* of Satan.

"This is the work of Tuck Fryer," grumbled an elderly gentleman who fell in beside the marshal.

"Vat makes you so smart?" Dill asked.

The man pointed to the caduceus design on his *keepah*. "I've got an education. Plus, I saw the Sabbath goy running away. He is one of them."

This man had to be the renowned Doc Challahday. His cure for chronic *greps* was known even as far as Fort Hamilton Parkway.

✡ ה ✡

"Vy vould dey set fire to the saloon?" Dill asked.

"That's where the ox apples are processed," Challahday replied. "We make Sabbath wine in one vat, fertilizer in the other."

"Manureoschewitz," Dill commented.

Doc and Dill watched as the firefighters extinguished the blaze.

"I was coming to welcome you to town," Doc said, "and to tell you that something has to be done about these *shtarkers*."

"You know de way to dis chicken ranch?"

"*Tahkeh*, it's right behind the saloon—" Doc began, then stopped. "Oh, you mean the ranch of the bad guys—the Fryers' Club. That's a half-day's ride due south." He chuckled. "I thought you wanted a *shtup* before heading out."

When the fire was under control, Dill went to where Radish was hitched. "*Es tut mir bang*. You'll have to wait until *Shabbas* to rest."

The horse also understood a little Yiddish and whinneyed that there was no need to apologize.

"Marshal Dill!" Miss Kitsel cried, hurrying over.

Dill hadn't seen a Jewish woman move so fast since his mother chased him around the apartment with an enema bag when he was three.

"It's a long ride," she said breathlessly. "You'll need this."

Miss Kitsel handed him a picnic basket. He looked inside. There was a wineskin filled with grape juice she'd taken from the children's table, and a checkered red and white napkin, which he opened gingerly. Three triangular pastries were crushed inside. Traces of prune filling stained the cloth.

"Hamantaschen," he said. "Vell, at least I von't be blocked like de oxen."

"Be careful out there," the young woman said, kissing his forehead. He hadn't been kissed there since he was three either.

Placing the nosh in his saddlebag and slinging the wineskin over the pommel, he handed the basket to Miss Kitsel just as Nu came running over. The former deputy was carrying the vest. Dill thanked him and slipped it on.

"Your brother does good vork," Dill remarked.

"Thanks. He said if you're shot, he'll fix the holes for free."

"At that price, I'll make sure I get ventilated!" the marshal winked as he climbed into the saddle.

Dill loped to the tax office where all the local records were kept. After finding what he wanted, the marshal made for the Santa Fe Trail. He could see the distant dust clouds of wagon trains as they headed west. He saw buzzards circling. He wondered if pioneers were considered *traif.*

Stopping several times to water the horse, it was sunset before Dill reached the gates of the Fryers' Club. The sky was bright red, and the spread below looked impressive. In fact, it looked like vermilion.

Tying Radish to a cactus, the lawman headed toward the main house. Golden candlelight burned in the window and chickens squawked in the barn. It could have been the old country, except for the wooden crosses on the family plot. And the fact that there was a family plot instead of a ditch.

As the marshal neared, the wind carried the odor of belched pork; Dill reflexively drew his gun.

"Mister, I've got a 40-40 trained on you," a voice cracked from somewhere to his left. "Don't take another step."

"Does dat mean backward, too?" Dill asked, instinctively looking for a loophole.

"Shut up!" the voice said. "Who are you and what do you want?"

Dill decided not to point out the contradiction in those last two statements. "I am de new marshal. If you are Tuck Fryer, I vant you should compete fairly vit de Nudgers and also don't set any fires."

The man laughed. "Forget it, sheriff. You can't beat Jews honestly!"

That made Dill angry. "I'm a marshal, not a sheriff."

"What the hell's the difference?"

"One is federal, the other is county, *shmendrick*," Dill replied. "Now you've got five seconds to surrender or face such *tsuris*—"

"*Har!*" the man snorted. "My carbine's got range over your .45!"

"Dat may be true," Marshal Dill replied. "But I can shoot de candle in your window, burn your house down, and de vay de vind is blowing guess what burns then? Your coop. And who do you think is your insurance underwriter?"

"Huh?"

"It's Stein & Stein out of St. Louis—I had a look. You just try and collect!"

The man swore. "See what I mean? You people don't play fair! It's like tryin' to chew with one tooth!"

Dill snickered.

"What's so funny?" Fryer demanded.

"De rebbe was right!"

"What the hell are you talking about?"

"You vouldn't understand," the marshal replied. "So? Ve got a deal?"

"What choice do I have?"

Marshall Dill returned to Nudge City with a promise from Fryer not to interfere with the local commerce.

"Such a mitzvah!" Miss Kitsel gushed when the lawman returned to town the following morning. "And you did it without firing a single shot!"

"*Avadeh*," he shrugged. "If you've got a *Yiddisha* cop, you don't need a gunshmuck!"

She Wore a Yellow Shmatta

Fort Apatsch was a spanking-new outpost on the banks of the San Hedrin River in the southwest Arizona territory. Built during the summer of 1867, it was the home of Gimel Troop, a melting pot of the roughest Hebrews west of Jericho, New York. The only time they weren't fighting among themselves—over Torah, over drinking from the same canteen without washing the mouthpiece, and whether it was right to fire a gun on Shabbas— was when they rallied to deride the goyim with a hardy, *"Kish mein tuchas!"*

Yet for all the *tsimmis*, they were destined to be remembered for the *naches* they gave their new leader, Captain Yankel Rosen.

Rosen went to Fort Apatsch straight out of West Point. He was sent to replace Commander William S. Hartsvaitik, who resigned his commission to open the Mesadika Music Hall, a Yiddish theatre in nearby Jewcson. Rosen was not only green, he was married to Kelly Greene of County Cork.

The men and their Indian guides did not know this as they watched the couple ride across the plains and through the gate, Captain Rosen in his dust-covered blues and the fair-skinned Kelly in a calico dress and big white bonnet tied tightly against the wind.

When a sudden gust carried away the yellow *shmatta* she wore around her shoulders, she asked her husband to grab "the shawl."

The onlookers muttered in unison, "A *shiksa!*"

Rosen did as his wife instructed.

"That means he's probably Jewish," observed Sergeant Ace Yorkville.

Rosen brought the buckboard to a stop in the center of the compound. The youthful sergeant ordered a pair of privates to help Mrs. Rosen and see to the luggage. She asked them to be especially careful of a carpetbag that was among her belongings. As that was attended to, the sergeant saluted the new commander.

"Welcome to Fort Apatsch, sir," he said. "I'm Sergeant Yorkville."

"Yorkville? Is your father a cooper in Gary, Indiana?"

"He is, sir," Yorkville replied.

"He made a bathtub for my Tante Jenny," Rosen said.

"May I ask what Jenny's last name was, sir?"

"Certainly," Rosen answered. "It was Finkel. Why?"

"Just—uh, making sure," he replied.

"Of what?" Rosen asked.

✡ 🔟 ✡

"Why, that we had our facts straight," Yorkville *funfehed*. "So, sir. Was your ride uneventful?"

"Well, we had a run-in with a hunting party of Mishigossi outside of Humboldt, but they were only hunting for bargains," Rosen replied. "They wanted something like my wife's yellow *shmatta*."

"I can understand why," the sergeant replied. "It's such a lovely shawl."

The men tittered behind them and, after a puzzled glance from the commander, Sergeant Yorkville hurriedly showed him to his quarters. There, Adjutant Lebediker was waiting.

"Sir!" the young aide saluted smartly as Rosen and his wife entered. "How are the captain and his *goyisha* wife—?"

Rosen shot Lebediker such a look, it straightened his *payas*.

"I'm so s-sorry, sir," the adjutant sputtered. "With respect, I meant to say *haimish* wife, for she looks so kindly—"

"Sergeant, have the bugler sound assembly," Rosen bellowed.

"At once, sir. For a minyan?"

"General assembly," Rosen snapped. "I've seen the uneasy glances since we arrived and heard all of the comments. I want it stopped!"

"I'll assemble the men, sir!"

Yorkville left and Rosen motioned for Lebediker to follow him. When they were alone, the captain turned to his wife.

"I'm sorry you had to hear that," he said.

"Hear what?" Kelly replied, as she was still wearing the bonnet.

"Nothing," the captain smiled. They walked to the doorway where he planted a kiss on her pale, freckled cheek. "Why don't you unpack. I'll join you as soon as I can."

Commander Rosen left, unaware that he and his wife were being watched by six sets of covetous eyes. Unhappy with the outlet store in Humboldt, the Mishigossi had stopped at the fort to trade. When Chief Chato's Lantsmen saw Kelly's yellow *shmatta*, they knew they had to have this woven sunshine for their leader's squaw.

Rosen addressed the men. While he spoke grandly about the evils of prejudice and stereotypes, the Indians left the canteen—slightly drunk and muttering "How" at everyone they passed. They entered the commander's quarters where they offered to buy Kelly's *shmatta*. When she refused their beads and gold—thinking they had offered her "beans from Golds"— they told her to come to their camp where they would share powerful medicine to make her husband's broken wind go silent.

"Show me this miracle, and you'll have as many shawls as you wish," she declared.

Not wishing to tip her husband off to her plan, Kelly left unobtrusively with the six Mishigossi.

In fact, the unscrupulous Indians had no such remedy. When they reached the settlement, the astonished chief offered to trade Kelly even more "beans from Golds" for the *shmatta*, and a mink skin to replace it.

"Do I look Jewish?" she said. "I'm keeping my shawl!"

Unfortunately, Chief Chato's wife, Shoulders That Burn, had already seen the garment and desired it. The Lantsmen had no choice but to take Kelly prisoner and seize the *shmatta*.

Back at Fort Apatsch, Commander Rosen finished his speech with two quotes.

"Prejudices, it is well known, are most difficult to eradicate from the heart whose soil has never been loosened or fertilized by education," he said, citing Charlotte Brontë, a quote which failed to register for many reasons; and one from his grandfather Isaac: "*Shtup ir!*" which resonated somewhat better.

After dismissing the men, Rosen returned to his quarters to find Kelly gone.

"Or is it to not find Kelly here?" he wondered, having spoken nothing but Yiddish until he enlisted to fight in the Civil War. There he was assigned to the all-gentile, tough-as-nails seventh Cavlary.

Learning from Lebediker that a group of drunk Mishigossi had been in the fort, Rosen remembered how they had coveted his wife's *shmatta*.

"A *broch*," he muttered.

The Mishigossi were a peaceful tribe, a branch of the Sioux, who took their namesake literally and preferred litigation over combat. They drove the U.S. government crazy, especially their chief attorney Chazzer Horse. Right now, however, the only "suits" Rosen cared about were the blues of Gimel Troop. Grabbing his wife's carpetbag, he headed for the stockade. There, at his command, a detachment was hastily organized.

"Men, I have reason to believe that my wife has been abducted by the Mishigossi," Rosen said. "We are going to rescue her."

There was a noticeable lack of enthusiasm as the troops assembled to the left of bugler Hertzich. One man, Private Laidik, moved so slowly his new wife had a full head of hair by the time he fell in. But Commander Rosen was unperturbed.

"Because our unit is new, we do not yet have regimental colors," the captain went on. With a flourish, he opened his wife's carpetbag and withdrew a piece of cloth which he showed to the men. It was a large white pennant with a blue gimel in the center. "My wife was going to present this to us on our first sortie. Since she is not here, I do so in her stead."

The unit oohed and ahed and mazeled as the captain attached the flag to his saber and handed it to Hertzich. It was the most beautiful embroidered gimel the men had ever seen, much nicer than the army-issued *tallis* bags.

"Bugler—sound the advance!" Rosen whooped.

Hertzich hesitated. Then, instead of "My Yiddisha Mama," he began to play "Tura-Lura-Lura." Moments later, the men joined in singing. For an instant, Rosen felt as though he were back in Killarney, many years ago, his mother singing a simple little ditty as she made latkes on the potato farm they owned. It was a sliver of land between warring Catholic and Protestant villages, and her greatest wish was that one day the Jews would have a homeland so they shouldn't know from such tsuris.

The horses headed west at a cantor, who had seen the Indians go by and pointed out the direction. Yankel Rosen's eyes fixed on the plumes curling from the smoke holes of the distant teepees. The smell that reached his nostrils was not the familiar shmaltz of the traditional Mishigossi chicken soup. It was corned beef and cabbage.

"They're making her cook for them!" the captain said through his teeth. He drew his carbine from its holster and raised the weapon high. "Charge!" he cried.

One day, that command would apply to purchases made at Saks. Today, it was a call to glory. Bugler Hertzich sounded the fanfare and, sabers in hand, the soldiers of Gimel Troop raced across the rugged plain. They stormed into the Mishigossi settlement, seeking vengeance for the abduction—and ears of corn for the regimental sukkah.

What they found surprised them. All of the Mishigossi—men, women, children, and dogs—were lying on the ground, knees to their chests, moaning in pain. In their midst stood Kelly, hands on hips, a half-smile on her red lips. The yellow *shmatta* was still wrapped around her shoulders.

"I knew their Siouxish-Jewish innards would respond to my cabbage as yours did the first time," Kelly said proudly.

Rosen slid from his saddle. Waving his hand briskly before him, dispelling the air thick with the odorous discomfort of the Indians, he embraced his wife.

"The Mishigossi are now like pony soldiers," Commander Rosen laughed. "All around them are *fortz*."

The troops roared and waved their pennant and gave the captain's lady a hip, hip, hurrah.

They left the Mishigossi where they had fallen, later sending the medic with Bromo and a bill, which hurt far worse than *der gaz*.

That night, Gimel Troop organized a proper welcome for their new commander and his lady, taking them to see the inaugural production of *Gai Cactus Offen Yam* at the Mesadika Playhouse.

When the revue was finished, and everyone had gathered outside, Kelly said, "It was very entertaining, but where was the sweet potato?"

The troops laughed and Commander Rosen kissed his wife as her yellow *shmatta* fluttered in the cool breeze. And the fame of that garment was destined to grow, for watching to the side, William S. Hartsvaitik began to hum as the yellow rose off *tsatskeh*. . . .

The Good, the Bad, and the Meshuganeh

It was June of 1847 when the Man With No Keepah came through the desert on a horse with no name.

"I think I'll call you Silverman," he said to the white steed as they reached the outskirts of Farshvitst, Texas.

It was the end of a long and arduous journey that began with a sea voyage from the Holy Land, which deposited him in Houston. There, he purchased the stallion as well as a chest, which he lashed behind the saddle.

The tall, lean *shtarker* hoped the trip would be worth it. He had an idea for a new kind of shul, and the open spaces of Texas called to him like the wilderness to the Old Testament prophets. His childhood friend Tuchas had a business in El Petseleh, and the Man With No Keepah would stay with him while building the temple. His goal was to finish by Pesach, two weeks hence.

It was a happy reunion for the two young men, who hadn't seen each other since Tuchas was a boy and had gotten lost searching for the *afikomen*. He had followed the smell of matzo which turned out to be a taco, a mistake that put him on a frigate bound for Mexico.

Tuchas was as good a businessman as he was a finder of unleavened breads. He went to work for a hangman, which he thought meant going to people's houses and putting up pretty pictures in nice frames. He learned otherwise and made nooses for an executioner after which—for after all, he was a Jew—Tuchas moved to the Hebrew settlement to work in the garment business, manufacturing neckties. Unfortunately, as the male population and the temperature both hovered around 105, there were not a lot of those to be sold. Moreover, while the hasids buttoned their collars, they did not wear ties.

"But with your new shul, our town will grow!" Tuchas exclaimed as he welcomed his childhood friend to his modest Log B'Omer cabin. "I will stock string ties for the cattle barons and Indian bolo ties for tourists and for the bubbes there will be bowtie noodles!"

However, as word of the soon-to-be-built shul spread, a pair of elders from the rich upper east side of town came to meet the self-proclaimed prophet. The men stood at the front of the wooden frame, though it wasn't the skeletal structure that held their attention.

"You!" one of them said through a beard that had flecks of potato salad near the white roots. "You, building the *shul!*"

The Man was on a ladder. He looked down. "Shalom!"

"*Gai pishen oyf der vant!*" the newcomer replied, which was ironic. The shul-builder was already facing a wall, and he did have to pee. "Where is your yarmulka?"

"I am the Man With No Keepah," he replied as he descended the ladder. "The Man for short."

The pair of hasids looked like they would *plotz*.

"Sacrilege!" the eldest elder cried. "A Jew must show his devotion to God!"

The skullcap-challenged man stepped up to the others. He pulled a cigarette from his shirt pocket and held up a match.

"I'd strike it against my phylacteries," he said, "but you may have noticed, I don't wear them . . . not even for morning prayer!"

"He called them phylacteries and not *tefillin*!" screamed the youngest elder, holding his ears and rocking his head from side to side.

The Man lit the match on a rail.

"*Oy, oy, oy!*" wailed both elders when they noticed pork jerky drying on the rough-hewn pine.

"Quit your kvetching," the Man said around the cigarette. "See, I've got this idea about Judaism that's different from what you folks believe on the banks of the Rio G'vir. I believe that as long as they're *mensches*, a man—or a woman—can worship in their own way."

"A woman!" the eldest elder shrieked. "You're no Jew!"

"But I am," said the Man, blowing smoke. "I'm what you'd call a Reform Jew!"

The Hasids' ears began to bleed.

"We will not tolerate breaking with tradition!" wailed the younger elder. "You will pay!"

"Wholesale?" the Man asked.

"He jokes!"

"We are important men!"

The Man just shrugged. "Go ahead. *Macher* my day."

Shouting an unbroken string of "*Kain ein horeh*," the hasids vowed to return after the next day, which was the Sabbath, and shuffled off.

"Was that wise?" asked Tuchas, who had come out with a selection of ties draped across his arm. Even though the men didn't wear them, he was going to suggest that they make very nice gifts.

"Wisdom is like a raven that comes to earth at the smell of carrion—you can't control it," the Man replied. "At least, according to this German fella Nietzsche."

"Well, he sure understands hasids," Tuchas said, then sighed. "They'll be back, you know. With help."

"Don't worry," the Man said as he went back to work building his shul. He glanced toward the desert and then toward the heavens. "I have help, too."

The man continued to work on the shul, cutting more lumber in the east wood and hauling it to town. Even with the elders gone, God continued to test him, sending such a sunburn to his unprotected *kop* that you shouldn't know. Still, he stuck to his vision and continued to work until sunset.

"What will you do tomorrow?" Tuchas asked over dinner, which was a party platter he snuck out from the Mendelbaum shivah. The pastrami was fatty which, as it happens, was why one of the butcher's customers had called him out and shot him. You don't try and cheat Bulvan Bill Cody.

"I intend to continue working," the man informed him. "God may have needed to rest on the seventh day, but not me."

"Wow!" Tuchas said. "You don't care who you piss off!"

The Man smiled. "Didn't you break one of God's Commandments by stealing these cold cuts?"

"They would have gone to waste!"

"Just like the Sabbath," the man said.

Tuchas sat there, his cheeks full of deli; his mouth puckered, as he considered what the Man had said. Then he said, "This time they'll come with their mothers, wives, and tantes. They'll nag."

"No," the Man assured him, chewing thoughtfully on a kosher pickle. "They'll ask me a question, thank me, and then they'll go."

"The sun has fried your brain," Tuchas opined.

The Man With No Keepah just grinned.

The next morning, the Man rode out to the desert with the chest he had purchased in Houston. He dug a hole, put it in, then covered it over and returned to El Petseleh to continue building his shul.

At sunset, while working on the roof, he noticed a torchlit procession headed in his direction.

"The Yahrzeit Candles of Death!" Tuchas shouted when he saw them coming. "They've come to burn you out!"

The Man climbed down and stood at the front of the shul, Tuchas behind him. The group stopped and the leader stepped forward.

"Man With No Keepah!" shouted the attorney, who introduced himself as the will elder. "We demand that you stop this *narishkeit!*"

"Why is it foolishness to build a house of worship?"

"You have no chicken, yet you claim to make chicken soup!" complained a *ballabosteh*.

"Can you not also make soup from matzoh balls or mushroom barley?" the Man shot back.

"It will not cure the *krenkheit!*"

"But what if I am not sick, just hungry?" the man asked. "I merely offer a different kind of Judaism, just as you will have a different kind of Pesach this year."

"What do you mean by that?" the *ballabosteh* snapped, charging from the group, elbow fat shuddering as she loomed larger and larger. As she approached, Tuchas wished he had a slingshot.

"I mean that on my way here I bought every Haggadah in Houston," the Man informed her.

"Even the expensive leatherbound ones?" asked the elder.

"All of them," the Man replied. "I buried them in the Ligindrerd Cemetery outside of town."

"We must go there!" shouted the attorney.

"And do what?" the Man replied. "Only I know which grave they are in."

A collective gasp rose from the group.

"He's got our Haggadahs!" cried one.

"He defiled a grave!" cried another.

"He's got money to buy leatherbound," remarked a third.

The only sounds to be heard for a long while were the rustle of the desert breeze, the flutter of the torches, and Colorado Zion singing about the confrontation from his porch down the street.

"This is blackmail," hissed the *ballabosteh*.

"Actually, it isn't," said the Shammes, wagging a calloused finger. "He hasn't asked for anything. It's more along the lines of a Talmudic lesson—"

She hit the sexton with a large wooden spoon.

"I say we dig up all the graves," barked welder elder, the blacksmith.

"And multiply his sin a hundredfold?" cried the will elder. "No." He regarded the shul-builder. "You handle with care. What do you want for the Haggadahs?"

"Something all Jews should understand," he answered.

"The humor of Myron Cohen?"

"The right to exist," the Man replied.

The hasids were very, very still. The uneven torchlight cast shadows that were dancing a hora.

At last, the eldest elder sighed. "I suppose there are different Jews in all of us," he said, taking their defeat as a sign from God.

The Shammes wept. He wished to be rid of his shameful actions.

One after another the hasids doused their torches in the dirt. This wasn't very smart, it being night. Tuchas had to run inside for a lantern before someone stepped on a nail or fell in a hole.

"Have the blacksmith come by at sunrise," said the Man With No Keepah. "I will deliver unto him the Haggadahs."

The next morning, the welder elder and the Man With No Keepah rode to the cemetery, passing the headstones of Mark Steinmetz, Mark David, and Mark Marx before finally reaching an un-Marked grave. Together, they disinterred the chest and rode back to town. When they arrived, they found the Hasids gathered with hammers and saws.

"We have come to help you finish your shul," said the youngest elder.

The Man With No Keepah smiled as he dismounted. "Isn't that too Amish?"

"A *bisl*," he admitted. "But at least they wear prayer caps."

Everyone laughed, including the Man himself. And well he might. For in the end, the hasids had been reformed.

The Ballad of Davy Kronsky

Born on a mountaintop on Tisha B'Av
Saddest day of the year—oy, lo tov.
  Named for his uncle, a man called Dov,
He had a manifesto from the Man up above.
Davy . . . Davy Kronsky.
Balnes *of the wild frontier.*

Tennessee in the 1820s was as untamed as a Lubavitcher's beard. Famed pioneers like Pishochs Bill and Daniel Bohmer were two-fisted and the Jews were simply tight-fisted.

The settlers of Bronfen, Tennessee, were no different from the rest, which is why they considered young Davy Kronsky a *muttelmessig*. He believed that if Jewish pioneers were to survive, goods and political power and resources must be shared equally.

"After all, if I am a *putznasher*, does that not make my

brother a *putznasher* as well?" he asked his mother when he was only three. Ethel Kronsky washed his mouth with a strong soap made from chicken fat. She said that the doctor he would one day become must not say such things.

Sobbing inside, young Davy kept the *farkuckt* cake of soap and vowed, one day, to kill that bar.

Unhappy with the oppression being visited upon his people, Davy left home when he was seven and lived in the woods, where he knew every *traifener bain* who hid in the wilds to enjoy an occasional shrimp salad or cheeseburger. Over the years, Davy developed muscles like Samson, survival skills like the Maccabees, and a philosophy of collectivism not unlike Karl Marx. Directed by the Lord—who spoke to him through a burning campfire, which seemed like not such a miracle to everyone but Davy—he built a kibbutz for pioneers, pilgrims, and those weary of oppression.

One day, it came to pass, over a dozen women of the nearby Shoshana tribe asked for sanctuary.

"What's the problem?" Davy asked, stressing the first syllable rather than the second, since the Indians did not speak Yiddish.

"Davy," said one, "we are being—how do you say it?—*noodged* by some very bad men."

"Yes, I heard the IRS opened an office in Bronfen."

"No," the woman said, then proceeded to explain that a brutish keelboat captain by the name of Mike Finkelstein had moored his vessel on the Red River and was charging tolls on every raft, canoe, and swimmer who passed.

"The Red River is sacred to us," said the squaw. "It has been free for as long as the oldest of us can remember."

"Old Where Is My Medicine Bag cannot remember what she did the night before," another of the maidens pointed out.

"Not like Spread Eagle," the others tittered, pointing to their spokesperson.

"I will see that it is freed from capitalist encumbrances," Davy promised, making a point to find out exactly where Spread Eagle made her tent, so he could report his progress.

Donning his coon-kishkeh yarmulka, Davy set out with his shotgun Baitsim. He had heard of this Mike Finkelstein, the son of an infamous *klipah* captain and a member of the seafaring Miami Finkelsteins. He had a reputation for violence, like his own *zeide Dov* looking for a shul seat on Rosh Hashana.

Davy took a shortcut through the woods, one which carried him past the hut of George Russeloff, Torah scribe.

"Davy!" he cried, ducking under rows of cowhide which hung drying in the sun. "What brings you here? Need more *mezuzahs* for the ol' kibbutz?"

"No," answered the young Marxman. "A river rat named Finkelstein is shaking down women who use the waterway."

"The pushy *pushkeh* taker!" Russeloff exclaimed. "Let's teach him some Commandments!"

Russeloff grabbed his battle-tallis, which was lined with chain mail, and the men set out through more *druchas*, singing a song of the old country, Crimea River. They smelled the Red River long before they reached it, a mixture of damp old campfires, smoked whitefish, and drying socks.

They also smelled skunk. Mike Finkelstein was 6-foot-6 and hadn't bathed since he was two, saying he wouldn't go near water unless some *k'nocker* could knock him in. So far, that hadn't happened.

When Davy and Russeloff arrived, Finkelstein was standing on a raft demanding payment from a boy and his African-American pilot.

"How much do you want?" the boy asked.

"A fin, Huck," Finkelstein replied.

Davy fired a shot from his *Baitsim*. "How about—*gornisht*?" he yelled from the riverbank.

The dark-eyed brute looked over. "Who is the *mekler* that'll be gummin' his next words from around my fist?"

"It's I, Davy Kronsky, whose next words will be heard without a Mike in his face."

Finkelstein leapt ashore from the raft. "You're pretty sure of yourself," he hissed. "How about a race?"

"Sorry," Davy replied. "I am not a racist."

The African-American waved his appreciation as he poled the raft away.

"*Maidel*!" the big man roared.

"You'll regret calling me that," Davy cautioned.

"Start sayin' the Kaddish," Finkelstein advised Russeloff. "I'm gonna Shiva yer friend's timbers!"

Russeloff obliged. "*Yisgadal v'yiskadash sh'may rabo—*"

"Har!" Finkelstein barked as he stalked toward them. "He knows the score!"

"I sure do, and it's one to nothing!" Russeloff shot back. "Boychick, the Kaddish is for you!"

Finkelstein turned the color of *charoset*, and one of his mighty paws flew forth. Russeloff happened to be nearest to the big man whose punch struck his chest. Finkelstein yelped as his knuckles struck the armored *tallis*.

Meanwhile, making like his namesake, Davy stripped off the coon-kishkeh *keepah* and held it by the tail. With his other hand, he scooped a stone from the banks and dropped it in the skullcap. He swung it round and round his head. After a half-dozen turns he let the rock fly. It struck Finkelstein square in the forehead, knocking him on his *tuchas*.

The *zetz* knocked his opponent out, so Davy and Russeloff took one leg each and dragged him into the river. The unfamiliar wetness caused the river rat to wake.

"A *mikveh* for the true *maidel!*" Davy laughed from the shore as Finkelstein splashed about.

"Is it Jonah or the whale?" Russeloff chuckled.

Finkelstein was not amused. Crawling onto the riverbank, he rose and ran toward Davy.

It was time for the *frum*tiersman to keep an old promise.

Reaching into a pocket, Davy withdrew the bar of soap his mother had used to wash out his mouth. He flung it in the path of the oncoming Finkelstein, whose wet foot came down on the slippery chicken fat. The pirate not only crushed it, he went tush over teakettle and landed hard on the muddy bank.

Davy stood over him. He pointed his trusty *Baitsim* at Finkelstein's chest.

"I know what you're thinkin'," Davy said. " 'Did he have time to reload or not?' Well, in all this excitement, I can't remember myself. But being as this has a percussion cap and can open a hole in you the size of a gefilte fish, you've got to ask yourself a question: Do you feel lucky? Well, do ya, putz?"

"Like Bugsy Siegel's left eye," Finkelstein replied, confident his answer would one day be funny.

"We have *der heskem* about this river?"

"I agree to let people pass."

"For free?"

Finkelstein nodded.

Davy handed *Baitsim* to Russeloff and helped the larger man to his feet.

"You've won," Finkelstein said, "but *Gott in Himmel* I must know—"

Russeloff grinned and fired at the retreating raft of the boy and his companion. He split the pole in twain, unaware how that would be funny one day, too.

Finkelstein reluctantly shook the hand of the man who had bested him. "From this point forward, Davy Kronsky has a friend in Mike Finkelstein," he said. "Whatever you need, just ask."

"You know," Kronsky said thoughtfully, "I'm thinking of

moving my *kibbutz* to Texas. I can get a good deal on an abandoned mission. Do you want to come?"

"Yeah . . . hmmm . . . I'll have to get back to you on that," Finkelstein said, edging away.

"I hear the Gulf is nice," Davy said.

"Y'know, I think I'll stay in Tennessee," the river rover remarked. "You might want to ask Jim Borer."

"The inventor of the kosher killing knife?"

"The same."

"Hokay," Davy shrugged. "Let me know if you change your mind."

"*Nit heint, nit morgen!*" Finkelstein waved. "Oh, and you might want to read up on Masada."

"Thanks," Davy said and turned to Russeloff. "He wasn't such a bad man."

"Just a schnorrer," Russeloff said, watching him slosh along the bank to his camp. "I wonder if I could have sold him a sealskin Torah mantel."

The men returned to the woods where Russeloff expressed some interest in going to Texas, though he heard it was really hot, and he was a *shvitzer*.

"It's *drai zich* heat," Davy assured him. "It won't slow you down."

Russeloff promised to think about it, and Davy returned to the kibbutz, where he delivered the good news to the Shoshana women. They thanked him for making such good medicine, which was nice to hear.

Davy was finally the doctor his mother had wanted.

You Call This a Bonanza?

It was nicknamed the Pitzvinik, and it was the smallest spread in the West. But in this case, size was misleading.

Officially, the Pitzvinik was the Bar Mitzvah Ranch, founded by Chaim Kashreit, the son of a New York butcher. Chaim had moved to the Nevada Territory in 1861, hoping to escape the humiliating stereotypes of his people. Indians had noses that were just as prominent, the Chinese were even more mistrustful of outsiders, and, in the ignorant, untamed West, he felt that, at the very least, no one would automatically associate Jews and money.

It was also true, being of late teenage years, that Chaim wanted to be as far from civilization as possible during the war between the States.

So he bought himself a half-acre outside Virginia City. He called it the Bar Mitzvah Ranch in honor of how he'd gotten the money to buy it, and he never intended to do more than raise a few chickens and grow some vegetables and live off the land. This was much as he had done in his backyard at home, since his father sold all the good cuts of meat at the shop, and there was only so much derma a boy could eat.

Now it happened that while planting a small garden to grow celery, lettuce, and bitter herbs, Chaim struck a shiny gold rock. He dug around it and found that he had discovered not just a nugget but a vein.

Running to the assayer's office in Virginia City—for a Jew can run when money, bargains, or National Socialists are involved—Chaim confirmed that what he found was gold. He filed a claim for what was soon to become known as the Chaimstock Lode.

While he was leaving, Chaim heard a comment that was typical of the joy and pain that afflicts every Jewish life:

"Boy, you people sure know how to make money!" growled a frustrated prospector who had been standing in line behind him with a thin pouch of gold dust.

"Gai platz!" Chaim replied, and the man thanked him kindly. "Well, that is an advantage to being among goyim," Chaim muttered.

Stepping outside, the young Jew was struck by a thought after being struck by a Chinese man who had been tossed from a laundry.

"I should hire someone trustworthy to do the actual digging," Chaim realized as he helped the young man to his feet after first making sure the fellow hadn't stolen his wallet. "Who are you?"

"My name is Hopalong Sing," the man replied. "I came to ask for the owner's daughter in marriage—but he will not give her to a penniless cook."

"Hoppy," said Chaim, "tell the old boy to prepare a chuppah!"

"What kind of dish is that?"

"One that comes with lots of white rice," Chaim said. "Friend, you're about to make some pennies."

The men went back to the Pitzvinik where they worked long hours, Hoppy shoveling and Chaim counting.

"You give golddigging a good name," Chaim told his sort-of partner, unaware of how that statement would one day come back to poke him in the *pipek*.

The gold piled up. Soon other miners bought up the land around the *Pitzvinik*, but none held more than a dusting of gold or silver.

"Boy," said a disgruntled neighbor, "you people sure know how to make money!"

Before long Chaim took a wife, who died; he took another, who also died; and then a third, who lived but ran off with a rock star, geologists being highly regarded in the West. He had a son from each of them: Akiva, Behaimeh, and Leibtsudekel Joe (who showed such an interest in rocks that Chaim wondered as to his origins).

The boys grew to manhood as Hoppy continued to dig, remarking at one point that if he went much deeper he'd be home. Yet while the Pitzvinik prospered, trouble brewed.

Living in a big valley nearby, widowed rancher Victoria Barklezzey had her eye on Chaim—or, more accurately, on the
Chaimstock Lode. She would come calling in an ornate black
buggy, which would have been the envy of the *chevra kadi-
sha*, bringing blueberry blintzes and sour cream.

"You are the answer to a prayer," she would tell Chaim as
they sat on the porch swing at night, listening to the coyotes
howl and the sound of Hoppy's shovel echoing from the bowels of the earth.

"If we stay together, you will have to become a Jew," he
replied.

"I am already a Jew, in here," the blonde *shikseh* touched
her heart.

"That's very nice," Chaim said, "but the Torah says *nisht
gut*."

"I have no idea what that means," Victoria smiled, "but I'll
do what I must to take your mine."

"Eh?" Chaim leaned closer. "Did you say 'take your mine'?"

"No, silly," she laughed. "I said 'make you mine!'"

"Ah," he replied.

"You silly man with your big nose!"

"Eh?" Chaim started. "Did you say 'big nose'?"

She laughed even harder. "I said, 'You silly man, you
should know!'"

Overhearing this from the terrace, the eavesdropping
Kashreit sons were filled with *chaloshes*.

"I don't trust her," said wise Akiva.

"Me neither," said Leibtsudekel Joe.

"Urp," said Behaimeh, who was also full of blintzes.

The boys decided to do something about it, though their efforts turned out to have the opposite effect. Sneaking out the back door, they sawed the wood tongue of Victoria's buggy more than halfway through. They had taken an abacus from Hoppy's room to calculate exactly when the tug of the horses would separate them from the carriage, causing it to spill down the steep dirt road leading down to the big valley, causing the wicked golddigger to plunge 450 feet to her death. Unfortunately, being Hebrew, they incorrectly read the abacus backward, causing the wood to break as soon as Victoria sat in the carriage. As a result, the woman had to stay the night. Because of this, their father got to eat fresh strawberry blintzes in the morning. All the boys but Behaimeh were upset.

Victoria continued to visit, and it wasn't long before Chaim asked for her hand. Akiva could have sworn he saw her give him just the finger, but said nothing. She converted by mail through the Famous Jews Yeshiva in Westport, Connecticut, after answering an ad that read, "Do you think you can doven?"

Meanwhile, the three Kashreit boys had enough. During a visit to Virginia City, they went to see Sheriff Roy Sanka, the most laid-back peacekeeper in the West. The Kashreits found him at the saloon.

"Don't you have anything on her?" pleaded Akiva over a warm beer.

"No," the sheriff drawled, "and you boys should keep your big noses out of this. Your pa knows what he's doing."

"But he's blinded by love," Behaimah countered—literally, since Sheriff Sanka was resting his lazy, whiskered cheek on the bar top.

"Got nothing, sorry," repeated Sheriff Sanka.

"Then he's misguided on account of his shlong," Leibtsudekel Joe rejoined—literally, since the frisky Kashreit boy had wandered off to check out a barmaid.

"Nope again," said Sheriff Sanka.

"Then papa knows something we don't," wise Akiva observed—literally, as he noticed his father going into the assayer's office. Victoria was not with him.

The boys waited until Chaim had left before heading back to the Pitzvinik. Though they were dying to ask about his visit, they said nothing. All had drunk way too much at the saloon and passed out before dinner.

The next afternoon was erev shabbas, and Chaim and Victoria were busy with paperwork when the boys roused themselves from sleep.

"Father!" Behaimah cried when he saw what was happening.

"*Farmach dos moyl!*" his father cautioned.

"But—"

"*Moisheh kapoyer!*" he yelled.

Akiva grabbed his brother by the elbow and pulled him toward the door. They were preceded by Leibtsudekel Joe, who had gone to the privy.

"Shmuck!" Behaimah growled. "He's signing over the mine to her!"

"Didn't you hear what he said?"

"Yes . . . ?"

"Moisheh kapoyer," said Akiva. "Mr. Upside-Down. I think he's telling us that things aren't what they seem!"

"Yes," Behaimah replied. "Our father is meshugga."

"No," Akiva said. "I think there's something else going on."

A few minutes later the couple emerged from the house. Victoria barely pecked her affianced on his cheek before hurrying off in her new buggy. His hands in his pockets, Chaim watched her go until all he could see was a sandy cloud— dirt, not the famed Indian comic. Then he wandered over to where the boys were standing.

"Pa, what's going on?" asked Leibtsudekel Joe.

"My three sons, I believe we've seen the last of that woman," Chaim replied.

"But I saw what you were writing," Behaimah said. "You signed away the rights to our property!"

"That's right, boy. And she gave us the rights to hers. We'll be moving to the big valley after shabbas. Then, I expect, she'll call off the wedding."

"Okay, I'm totally *farblondzhet*," admitted Leibtsudekel Joe.

"Tell them, Hoppy," Chaim said as Hoppy emerged from the low mine. The onetime cook liked the sound of those words and noted them in his noodle.

"The mine is prayed out," the Chinese worker smiled.

"You mean played out," Akiva corrected.

"No. I mean we prayed for more gold and didn't get it," Hoppy explained. "So, yes. Now it's played out."

"Victoria Barklezzey got a half-acre of bupkes while we got three hundred acres with something called rock oil," Chaim told them. "I checked with the assayer. If we build a well, we can refine it into kerosene, and who knows what else?"

The boys were impressed, and within a month they were pumping crude. Hoppy returned to Virginia City and opened The Low Mine Restaurant, which made him wealthy. And Sandy Cloud went to New York where he hosted a burlesque act for children. Only Victoria Barklezzey ended up *farpisht*, having called off the wedding as Chaim predicted. She spent the rest of her days sitting alone on the porch of the Pitz-vinik, staring into her dark, empty hole.

However she had come away from the experience with a lesson, one she would never forget: *Boy, those people sure know how to make money!*

Stagekvetch

They called him the Ringo Kiddish.

He was a bounty hunter who carried a Remington .44 in his right hand and a prayerbook in his left. If he had to put one down, it was always the firearm. The 29-year-old never ate a meal, went anywhere, shot anyone, without the appropriate *brocha*.

Things changed when Ringo met Dalit, the youthful owner of D-Kops, a booking agent for what were euphemistically called 'saloon girls'—but, in fact, the book she used was the Kama Sutra. The former dancer told Ringo she was tired of her lowdown life in Denver and yearned for the open spaces of a place like Dallas. Dalit convinced the gunslinger to settle down and buy a spread where she could help raise some other kind of meat, as well as a couple of *Kinder*. Seeing as how they had enough money between them, the Ringo Kiddish decided to give it a shot.

Only later did he realize the shot should have been buck.

✡ 50 ✡

As he prepared to board the stagecoach to Texas, Ringo wondered where Dalit could be. Heading over to the Rusty Shtupper Saloon, where she had an office, he saw Dalit helping a zaftig woman out the front door. He thought it was very kind of her to be helping this old *nafkeh*. From the wrinkled looks of her, she had probably been on her back since Herod was king. No doubt she was one of the less expensive purchases one could make from D-Kops, perhaps for as little as a hard-boiled egg.

Dalit smiled when she saw Ringo.

"*Tateleh*," she said to her intended, "I'd like you to meet my mother, Dybbuk."

The words hit Ringo so hard he felt pain in his phantom foreskin. He snapped from his stupor just enough to extend his right hand in welcome.

"You shake like a *faigeleh*," the woman sneered, her nostrils expressing displeasure with a horse-like flaring.

It was the only time in his life Ringo wished he had put down the prayerbook and held onto the firearm.

"Mother, Ringo is a gentle man," Dalit reminded her.

"Soft hand, soft *shvantz*," Dybbuk croaked.

Behind her, Ringo noticed Deputy Shemp Wilcox standing in the window of the sheriff's office and pointing vigorously at a wanted poster he held in his hand. The lawman's lips formed the words, "It's not too late!" The bounty hunter read the broadside, about a plumber who killed people by blowing up outhouses. There was a $5,000 reward. Ringo suspected he would probably have to deal with less shit if he went back to work. It was tempting.

"Mother, why don't you get on the stagecoach while Ringo and I get your trunks," Dalit suggested.

"Why such a rush?" she asked. "So the outlaws ahead shouldn't get bored?"

"The coachman has a schedule to keep," Dalit said as she helped her mother up the step.

"He's already a day late," Dybbuk replied, glaring up at the driver. "Another two minutes won't kill him."

"It might kill you, Grandmaw," the burly Kuck muttered from the driver's box, twisting the reins into a tight, ugly shape.

After Dybbuk had settled in with her knitting—"Tell the driver he should try not to bump so much when we leave," she remarked, ignoring the noose dangling outside her window—Dalit took Ringo aside.

"You look pale," she said, which was quite an achievement for a man who had spent twenty of his thirty years in the bright Western sun and was still standing directly under it. "The ride will do us all good. Mother just needs a little time to get to know you."

"You said nothing about a mother," he replied dismally.

"What did you think, I came down the Colorado River in a basket?"

"I meant a mother with us."

"What should I do, leave her here?"

That sounded like a good idea, and if the street weren't such a pig wallow, he would have dropped to his knees and begged. Instead, he said a *brocha* popular among kosher butchers, not sure who was the *shochet* and who was the cow.

"It will be good to have mother in Texas," Dalit went on, unencouraged. "She will help to make our clothes, cook our meals, and babysit."

The last was important. Ringo knew he would want to get away from Dybbuk like the Hebrews from Pharaoh.

The three passengers were joined by Doc Boozer, a young lush and a gentile who nonetheless caught the eye of Dybbuk as an alternative to my-son-the-gunslinger. They had a lively conversation, if "lively" is defined as Dybbuk talking nonstop and Doc being passed-out with his head against Ringo's shoulder. The newly retired bounty hunter said a *brocha* asking for God to pass Doc's oblivion to her. In fact, if they weren't so late, he'd have asked Kuck to stop the coach and let him get the medicinal laudanum he'd packed. The contents would have gone directly from his chest into Dybbuk's chest.

The coach reached Dodge City by nightfall. There, Ringo checked to make sure that there wasn't a bounty on Dybbuk before retiring. The following morning they set out with one additional passenger, a gambler named Hat Feldman. He got his name because he was never without his stovepipe hat. He always wore it because of the derringer he carried in a secret compartment on top.

Feldman was introduced around, his eyes lighting on the former madam.

"Hello, Dalit," he leered.

His expression changed from lust to revulsion when he was introduced to her mother.

Dybbuk eyed Feldman, too. She had a weakness for cards and taught him Canasta. By the end of the second day of travel, Feldman had made $100, not because he enjoyed a game played with 104 *farshtunkener* cards but because Ringo slipped him a ten-spot every hour he kept Dybbuk busy.

The third day found them on the last spur of the journey, swinging through the plains outside Ada, Oklahoma. This happened, by unfortunate coincidence, to be the name of Dybbuk's sister, the *oisgeshtrobelt* wife of a banker. She didn't have the time of day for a poor younger sibling who not only didn't marry rich, but wed a barber who eventually ran off with a Pole. Dybbuk stopped playing cards and complained openly for the better part of the day.

Fortunately—since death was proving the better option than continuing to Dallas—this region was home to the no-torious Apache comedian Geronimo Howard. His failure to make it as a comic actor in the white man's theaters had sent him on a vicious tear through the plains, what he and his supporters called the "I'll Give You a Reason Not to Laugh" raids. The route followed by Kuck happened to bring him right into the traveling band of Apaches. No sooner did they see the coach than they were on their ponies and screaming about scalps.

✡ לב ✡

"Ticket brokers had nothing to do with the low turnout!" Kuck shouted as he reined the team to a gallop.

But the Apaches couldn't hear him above their war cries or the screams of Dybbuk.

"*A klog iz mir, a klog iz mir!*"

After a minute of listening to this, the gambler reached for his derringer and put it to the woman's temple.

Dalit put herself between them. "Stop!" she cried. "Shouldn't you hold off until the Indians are actually upon us?"

"Why wait?" Feldman said, pushing her aside and pressing the barrel deep into over-powdered flesh that smelled like the strong roses used to freshen an outhouse.

"Whoa, I'll take that pea-shooter," Ringo snarled, grabbing the gun.

"Sure thing—you have dibs, I guess," Feldman said.

But Ringo didn't shoot Dybbuk. He tucked the *stikeleh* "stocking gun" into his waistband and, saying a *brocha*, reluctantly left his prayerbook on the seat. He climbed to the top of the stagecoach. There, he drew his own .44 and trained the two guns on the pursuing Apaches.

"You'll never hit anything with those!" Kuck yelled.

Indian after Indian fell from his horse.

"Go now," the driver shrugged.

But it wasn't Ringo's shooting which caused them to drop. His shots had actually struck cactus, tumbleweeds, and Feldman. Behind the Apaches was a unit of cavalry, led by Lieutenant Blondjen, firing Springfield rifles.

"We must retreat," Geronimo Howard said to his son. "Too often have I died in the venues of the white man."

"First you give up greasepaint . . . now warpaint!" his son chided.

"Oh, you think comedy is easy?" Geronimo Howard shot back. "Try it, Windy Colorado Fields!"

With that, the chief broke off the attack, followed by the remainder of his war party. The stagecoach rolled into Dallas accompanied by Lieutenant Blondjen and his men.

"It's a good thing you were on patrol," Kuck said as he climbed down.

"You can thank this young lady," he said, dipping his hat to Dybbuk.

"Young Lady?" Kuck said to Ringo. "Maybe you did hit those Indians. This guy is obviously blind!"

"Not at all," the lieutenant said. "We found a canasta on the prairie. No one discards a hand like that unless they're in trouble. We know that because our commander is a devotee of the game . . . and of its players."

The group followed the young officer's gaze to Dybbuk.

"Ma'am, I believe that General Lord would want to meet such a courageous woman," the lieutenant went on.

"Lord," she said thoughtfully. "That doesn't sound Jewish"

"Exactly so," he replied. "The general changed it from Lordsberg to get a promotion. Anyway, his wife recently died of consumption—"

"A terrible disease," Dybbuk tsk-tsked.

"Actually, it was from consuming too much hazelnut almond cake with raspberry coulis," the lieutenant said. "Might I persuade you to be his dinner guest at the fort's inn?"

"It's not a very appetizing name, but I like the price," Dybbuk admitted.

While they conversed, Ringo acted quickly. He handed her bags to the troops, bought a horse and buggy in Dallas, opened a bank account, and took out a loan to buy property. He rode back with the banker so the lieutenant could notarize the papers, helped Dalit onto the buckboard, and was prairie bound.

"Thanks for everything!" he called over his shoulder, adding a *brocha* for the safe journey of his soon-to-be mother-in-law.

"Who was that meshuggeh man?" Lieutenant Blondjen asked the bank officer.

"Don't you know him?" asked the loan arranger. "That's Ringo Kiddish."

There was a double wedding that summer, and Ringo not only hung up his .44 and lived happily with Dalit but gave up the prayer book as well:

He couldn't stand the fact that whenever he prayed to the Lord, Dybbuk thought she meant her.

Chai Noon

"**D**o *not foreskin me, oh my darlin'* . . ."
The distant clop of hooves caused Marshal Will Kahane to stop playing his guitar. Setting the instrument aside and raising the pin-rolled edge of his Stetson, he crossed the stoop in front of the sheriff's office. He stepped over a Kickapoo Indian who was sleeping in the shadow of a trough and looked down Frankie Lane.

It was just the rabbi making a house call on the young Widow McCarthy.

Kahane returned to his seat. He did not resume playing. He picked once a day to keep his fingers nimble. A lawman needed that—especially this one, who was also the local *mashgiah*. Kahane had to inspect dozens of crates of meat coming to Pogrom, Kansas, each day. Lately, he had been turning away shipments from Frankfurter Miller, a powerful cattle baron, insisting that they were not kosher. Miller vowed to end the ban by noon this very day. Word in the shul was he had engaged a gang of Cossacks to change the Marshal's mind.

"And not through polite conversation and handling," warned his deputy, Harvey Pill, who found reasons to avoid just about every responsibility a deputy should undertake. For instance, he celebrated 372 Jewish holidays every year.

A fine-grain film of sand hung above the street, stirred by a constant wind from the east. Above it, the large clock outside the general store said 11:44.

Just then the wind carried the smell of *k'naidlech*, which preceded the arrival of Kahane's wife, Amy. She wore a blue ribbon in her hair and carried a *shissel* covered with a napkin.

"Almost lunchtime!" she said in a singsong voice.

Amy was a good-hearted girl, full of grace, but a bit of a *draikop*. His family had advised him against the marriage, Amy being 22 and Kahane scratching at 56. But she was cheerful and attentive and got along well with young Deputy Pill, which was important when Kahane had business in another town. His only regret was that she had no sense of humor, for the sheriff was a legendary punslinger.

"Tsatskehleh, some bad men are coming to kill me," Kahane said, rising and setting the plate on his chair. He took her small, fair hands in his. "I really have to watch for them."

"You shouldn't fight on an empty stomach," she said sternly. "In fact, you shouldn't fight at all."

"You oughta be with Deputy Pill," Kahane remarked.

"Shouldn't I at least wait till 12:01?" she asked.

"Pardon me?"

"Oh—uh, nothing," she said quickly, her cheeks flushing.

"I meant that he agrees with you. He thinks this fight is foolish. But there's more at stake than dietary laws. What happens if the Torah scribe decides to use pig hide, or the *tsitsis*-maker mixes linen and wool? What of our traditions?"

"Take it from me, you're pissin' up a drainpipe," said the Indian.

Amy held her husband tightly. "Pill said these Cossacks are professional killers, the same bands that helped to route Napoleon."

"Napoleon was 'desserted,'" Kahane quipped, the pun just sitting there like an over-greased latke.

"Will Kahane, don't try and sweet talk me," Amy chastised him, inadvertently punning back.

"Okay, Sugar," Kahane replied.

The clock said 11:51 and Kahane eased from his wife. "You need to go home, now," he told her.

She protested, her face ribboned with tears. She pulled at her hair, her ribbon faced with tears.

"What about our religious beliefs? The Ten Commandments, 'Thou shalt not kill.'"

"Actually, the verb used in the Torah is *ratsah*, which means 'murder,'" he said. " 'Killing' is okay—"

"*Gai avek* with your translations!" she snapped. "You told

my friend Mary that the Torah doesn't ban homosexuality, only man-rape."

"That's true—"

"But the Torah doesn't go on to say that women lying with women is a *mitzvah*."

"Not as such," the red-faced Kahane agreed. He glanced at the clock. It was 11:53. "Honey, I really have to prepare for battle."

"Let's just leave this town," she implored. "We can go live with Papa at the Oy Vey Corral."

Kahane touched the tin Star of David pinned to his vest and sighed, "Oh, to be torn twixt love and a paycheck!"

Realizing it was hopeless, the woman sobbed and unhooked her necklace. It was the gold chai her husband had given her when they became engaged. She went to fasten it around his leathery neck.

"Don't make me take this off your dead body," she said.

"I won't," he replied. "Though if I am killed, I want to be buried with it around—"

"*Chap nit!*" she said peremptorily. "That's 24 karat. You die, it's coming off."

"In that case, you'd better keep it," he said, removing the chain and putting the necklace back in its proper place.

Amy picked up the plate, raised the napkin, and once again offered her husband a *k'naidlech*.

"No, dumpling, thank you," he replied.

Wailing, the woman hurried down the street.

It was 11:55. Kahane checked his six-shooters.

"Och un vai," he thought sadly. It would be very nice to have six-shooters instead of just myself.

The marshal went back to his seat. He picked up the guitar and was about to continue singing when he heard horses snort at the end of the street. He peered in that direction and saw a line of big Mongol stallions, which announced the arrival of the Cossacks. Actually, only the four horses had arrived. The killers stumbled into town a full minute later, having fallen from their mounts following a vodka bender on the way to Pogrom.

It was 11:58. Marshal Kahane strode to the center of the street.

"Can I help you shikkers?" the lawman asked.

"What did you call us?" snarled one.

"Drunks," Kahane replied.

"Oh," the Cossack answered, relieved. "I thought you called us shiksas." The huge man wobbled from the pack, a scimitar in his big right hand, a bottle of vodka in his left. He raised the latter in salute. "We have come to kill you. L'Chaim!"

Kahane didn't bother to point out the tummler's oxymoron.

The other three Cossacks lined up beside their leader, all of them carrying the same big, curved swords. They ran forward.

It was 11:59.

Kahane drew his guns. He wondered how they were going to beat him if he had the six-shooters and all they had were four steel blades—

Just then, the two men on the end raised their swords and held them horizontally. The highly polished blades reflected the sun, blinding Kahane.

"That's how!" he exclaimed.

Shielding his eyes but refusing to give ground, Kahane squinted at his targets. He did not want to fire randomly, for if he hit a horse that would be killing.

The clock struck noon. Suddenly, there was a shout from the sidewalk.

"Leave my husband alone!"

Amy rushed forward, throwing *k'naidlech* at the Cossacks. The men turned to face this new threat. When they did, Kahane fired. Three of the attackers went down, deader than Catherine the Great's horse, but the fourth managed to reach the young woman. He drew his *kindjal* and put the dagger to her tender throat.

"Throw down your guns or I will open her like a wineskin!" the Cossack warned.

Amy was out of *k'naidlech*. She stared helplessly at her husband.

"Go ahead, Taras Bulba!" Kahane taunted. "Kill her! You die next!"

The Cossack hesitated. Amy shot her husband a look that shivered his *kishkes*. He winked in a way that told her I know what I'm doing. She scowled in a way that said she was going to sever his shlong.

Though three of his comrades lay dead, Cossacks do not like being bullied. They like being bullied by Jews even less. The traditional war cry, "Urrah," erupted from the warrior's mouth. His grip tightened and he was about to draw blood when Amy bit his hand, wrenched herself free, and delivered a devastating knee to the groin. The Cossack went down like a pair of empty pantaloons. No sooner had he hit the street than Deputy Pill scurried from the Kahane house where he was protecting Amy. Pill took the Cossack to jail while Amy stormed toward her husband.

"*Shain vi di zibben velten!*" Kahane exclaimed.

"Don't talk about my beauty!" Amy yelled. "What were you thinking?"

"*Neshomeleh*, the knife edge was on your chai," her husband said. "His blade would not have cut through it."

"Are you meshugeh?" she cried. "Gold is nothing! You could cut through with a dried herring!"

"*Gevalt!*" Kahane said. "Well then, God would have protected you."

She hit him on the side of the head with the *shissel*, which she still held.

"Is my name Isaac?" she yelled. "That *parech* would have killed me!"

"Okay, okay, so maybe I made a mistake," Kahane admitted. "What's important is that I didn't run from duty and you didn't forsake me."

"And—?"

He thought for a moment. "And you're not kaput."

Amy softened and embraced her husband. "What do you say we pack up now and leave Pogrom behind?"

"Good idea," he said. "We'll go anywhere you want."

"*Oy vey*," she replied.

"What's wrong?" he asked.

She seemed puzzled. "Nothing. I meant we'd go to Papa's corral."

"I know," he said, kissing her on the forehead. "When we get there, I'm going to teach you to crack jokes."

"And I'm going to teach you to break horses," she enthused.

"That was funny," he said.

"What was?"

"Crack . . . break . . . ," he replied.

She looked at him blankly and he shook his head as they walked home, his big hand moving his fair-eyed beauty along.

Nashville Katz: The Jews Singer

Nathan Katz was bored.

The *chazen* of the Orthodox Beth Hillel Shul was bored with ceremony, bored with tradition, and bored with the blank expressions he saw from the bimah.

In short, he was bored with his chosen profession.

The Katz family had come to St. Louis, Missouri, a century before, in 1764, with the first fur traders. The three brothers made so much money that one of their sons decided to balance the scales by serving God in relative poverty. That was Nathan's great-great grandfather, as fate would have it.

"Thank you very much, you *lemeshkeh* Litvak," Nathan thought so very often.

One day, while leading the large congregation in a chorus of *Chad Gadya*, Katz suddenly stopped. The assemblage, which had come to life during the refrain, now drifted into silence.

"Hillel is alive with the sound of music," the *chazen* said softly, then began to sing a capella, "with songs we have sung for five thousand years. Hillel goes to sleep with the sound of music. Such *kimpetoren* comes from the songs sung here."

The sea of black hats sat motionless. Several women swooned and Mrs. Tessie Katz and her husband, the retired *chazen*, glared at their son.

"My friends *yung un alt*," Nathan went on, "I believe there is a better way to spread Torah and the teachings of Judaism than by singing in shul."

"Since when does the *chazen* give *di droshe*?" the rabbi angrily demanded.

"This is not a sermon," Nathan said. "This is my way of saying shalom. I've decided I'm going off to spread the joys of Yiddish by becoming a country *krechtser*."

Still no one moved. Most of those who hadn't fainted were asleep and the rest were woolgathering. Some of those people were mentally selling that wool in a wondrous place called Seventh Avenue.

"What will you sing about?" his mother finally cried out, as opposed to simply crying.

"What Jews know better than anything else."

"A good value?" Tessie Katz wailed.

"No," Nathan replied. "I will sing of pain."

His eyes aglow with the strength of his conviction, Nathan left the shul. He did not even flinch when a siddur hit him in the back of the neck, though it hurt to hear his father compliment the rabbi for his aim.

"You can start by writing about that *zetz!*" Morton Katz yelled after him.

"I will use this throbbing as the beat of my first songs," the newly retired chazen promised himself.

Buying woodblocks to keep the distinctive horse-clop beat of country *krechtsing*, Nathan decided to head for Tennessee and make a new name for himself—literally, by adopting the *nom-de-plagen*, Nashville Katz.

Traveling on foot, Nathan stayed in cheap rooms where he wrote inspired melodies such as, "I Should Grow Like an Onion with My Tears in the Ground," "Achy, Breaky *Hitsik*," and "99 *Luftmensches*." By the time he reached his destination, he had more songs than the Confederacy had bad debts. After three months he reached his destination. It would have been better if his shoes lasted more than two months, but at least it inspired a song called "Barefoot in a Parka."

Nashville was growing after the war between the States: not Nashville the man, who was shrinking, not having eaten very well on the road. But Nashville the town. It had seen a population boom, a transportation boom with the coming of trains and mule-drawn streetcars, and now it experienced the boom of Nathan's woodblocks. The wandering Jew used what little savings he had to rent a small barn. He put up posters around town announcing a Jewbilee service, though the crack-crack-cracking of the woodblocks was advertisement enough. Most of the city's 25,000 citizens knew exactly where he was and stayed well clear of the area.

On the Thursday night that Nashville Katz made his debut, three people were in attendance. One was Nathan himself. Another was the woman he'd hired to run the concession stand. The third was the woman's nephew, who had been living in the hayloft of the barn when Nathan rented it.

After the concert had ended, a voice descended from above. "Friend, you have a problem!"

"I'll say," Nathan replied as he commiserated with his concessionaire. "We didn't sell a single box of Milk Duds."

"That's not it," the voice said.

"*Tahkeh*, you didn't pay for the cow," Nathan shot back.

"The problem is, you've got no soul."

"Thanks, Moishe Maven, but I'm not in the mood for a theological debate—"

"I'm talking about musical heart, not existential spirit," the man replied.

"Hey, I've got musical heart!"

"Funny," the man chuckled. "You don't look bluish."

Nathan walked to the overhang. "Let me see your mezzanine ticket."

"Didn't buy one. Wouldn't have." A black man stepped from the shadows. He looked about sixty years old. "Name's Apollo Johnson and when slavery got what-for, the boss let me stay on a while. So I worked a little, but mostly I sat up here and wrote songs."

"*Me ken brechen!*" Nathan sighed. "Another party heard from."

"Been doin' it all my life."

"Oh? What kind of songs do you write?"

"Ditties with titties, tunes with bounce," he answered. "You had a few good hooks there, singin' about 'Blue Suede Jews' and 'Jailhouse Rock of Ages.' But no one wants to listen to knock-blocks. They want something they can toe-tap to." The man picked up a banjo and shook off the straw. "They want to hear this."

Now, Nathan Katz had a stiff neck—right where the *siddur* had hit him—but he wasn't stupid. As the newcomer picked a tune, Nathan found his feet moving. It wasn't the Bottle Dance from *Fiddler*, but at least it was something.

When the musician finished Nathan said, "Mr. Johnson! How would you like to be my accompanist?"

"What kind of billin' would I get?" he asked.

"How does Nashville Katz and Black Katz sound?"

"Unlucky," he replied. "Let's just say Nashville Katz plays with A. Johnson."

Something didn't sound quite right about that, but Nathan agreed. The week following shabbas was a flurry of writing, rewriting, and rehearsing. One of the first things the former *chazen* did was to discard the blocks and, at Apollo's insistence, buy a ram's horn.

"Once in a while you should stop singin' and wail on that," Apollo said, feeling that some of the tunes should be shofar-driven.

"I'll be a regular Challah Parker," Nathan quipped.

For the next six days the country-*krechtser* felt as though he was back at the Yeshiva, except that it was a barn, not a school, and the rebbe was a *shvartze*. Also, what they were doing here was a lot more exciting than "Isaiah: the Prophet of Cleansed Lips" and "Messianic Apologetics 3."

The week passed quickly. During that time the concessionaire was also hard at work. When new posters went up—a broadside of a barn—they not only promised a new musical sensation but a fresh taste treat from the hardworking cook and her Jewish employer: Aunt Jemima's homemade latkes. Afraid that Tennesseans wouldn't know what that meant, the cook thoughtfully provided the subheading, "Jew cakes."

On the night of the concert, Nathan was surprised and delighted to see a mob of people waiting outside the barn.

"We did it!" he crowed to Apollo.

"Not yet," the songwriter pointed out. "We got their attention. Now we got to entertain them."

He was right. Nathan remembered the crowded but boring services, the droning sermons, and the endless receptions with cheesecake so heavy it could bend light. He remembered the failure of the concert the week before and the shame he would have to endure for the rest of his life if he had to return to Beth Hillel.

"Eye of the *tsiklen zich*!" he said to himself, focusing his energies.

The crowd filled the barn and an eager buzz filled the air. It was mostly men of questionable sexual orientation who seemed disappointed to discover that "A. Johnson" referred to a musician. They were stirred, however, by the Cajun inflected "Havana Gila," and were on their feet for the rousing "Waitin' for the Robert Aleichem." They sobbed for the heartfelt "My Yiddisha Mammy," and even enjoyed the soulful "Battle Haman of the Red *Pupik*."

> *Old King Ahasuerus wanted Esther for his bride.*
> *He had trampled all his* yentzen *and his shlong longed*
> *for a ride.*
> *He set loose the bloody Haman whom the Jews did not*
> *abide.*
> *That's Purim, for y'all.*

Nathan didn't win any converts that night, but he made a few friends. And for a Jew living in the South, that wasn't so bad.

"Now we did it!" Nathan said, embracing his partner after the show and handing him his share of the box office.

"It was a good start," Apollo agreed as he gathered up his things.

"Wait! What are you doing?" Nathan asked.

"Movin' on," he replied. "My work here is done."

"What are you talking about? We only played one gig!"

"I mean my farmin' and cotton pickin' work is done," he said.

"But what will you do?"

"Use this money, go to New York, and open a club," replied Apollo.

"I see. What will you call it—so I can look you up if I ever get there."

"Well, since I did my plannin' all those years I spent pickin' cotton, cotton, and more cotton, I think I'll name it, 'Shove That Lash Up Your Brown Eye, You Mutha.'"

Nashville nodded thoughtfully. From what little he knew of New York, that could work.

Word of the toe-tapping, soul-raising "Jews Singer" spread, not just among the gay community but throughout the goy community as well. Soon, Nathan outgrew the barn and the city built him a new hall, though they eventually changed the spelling from "Jewbilee" to "Jubilee." Aunt Jemima also changed the name of her griddle treats from "Jew cakes" to "Flap Jacobs," though it wasn't until the gay Republicans from Tennessee started making syrup that they really took off.

Nathan never returned to Beth Hillel, though many years later his parents came to visit him in Nashville. They had heard of his success, forgave his flight, and needed a few dollars to complete their own relocation to Miami. He gave it to them. He even saw them to the train.

As they were boarding, his father handed him a gift: the siddur that had struck his neck so long ago.

"Don't forget your roots," the elder Katz said.

Nathan never did.

After all, they gave him his first hit.

The Magnificent $7 (Marked Down to $5.98)

His name was Halava, and he was the fiercest desperado in Mexico. He and his band of thirty cutthroats would enter small villages, steal all but the barest necessities the peasants needed to survive, then return along the same circuit the following season.

One such town was Nuevo Maízo, home to thirty-odd corn farmers and their families. Tired of being pillaged year after year, they turned to the village elder for advice on how to fight these locusts in human form.

"Finally grew a pair, did you?" Señor Senior asked.

"No pears, just corn," said Jose, one of the three men who came to see him.

The elder sighed. "Never mind. You need to hire gunmen to protect the village."

"You mean hire Halava's men?" asked another man, Hernando. He shrugged. "I guess that makes sense. They will already be here."

The elder sighed again. "No. Go to the border. Hire gun-slingers who are not loyal to your enemy . . ."

"But we have no money," said the third, Chiquita, who was a little different from the other men.

"So stop in Shlakberg and borrow money from the Jews," Señor Senior replied. "It will be like dealing with Halava, but without the gunplay."

"That's a relief," said Jose.

"Not really," the elder said. "They will haggle you to death."

Told to negotiate by threatening to take their business elsewhere—"and use those exact words," the elder cautioned—the three villagers were given a diamond ring. The jewelry had belonged to the late Mrs. Senior—if one defines as "late" her having run off with Halava—and a mesh bag full of foil-wrapped chocolate coins.

Hernando looked at the sack. "Surely the Jews will not believe these are real money."

"No, but be sure to call it 'gelt' and show it to the children, who will nag their parents until they get the contents," Señor Senior replied. "The Jews will lend what you need just to get rid of you."

The men immediately set out for Shlakberg where their stay was brief, though not for the reasons they had expected.

The Mexicans heard there were seven Jewish gunfighters living in Shlakberg. They found the men on Bagroben

Hill, where they were interring members of the Nochshlep-
per Gang.

"What did they do?" Chiquita asked, boldly approaching
their leader Bris.

"They tried to distribute fake mah-jongg cards," he replied. "The *alter moids* pelted them to death with tiles."

"Bam! Crack!" laughed Barnarish, an axe-wielding luna-
tic with a trace of Indian blood.

Chiquita looked the group over. He counted only six and
learned that one of the Jewish gunfighters had moved to Pal-
estine so he could hang up his holster and live in peace. Still,
the remaining half-dozen looked tough. Better them than six
of another.

"I never thought I'd say this," Chiquita told Bris, "but I'm
looking for a man who's quick on the draw."

Bris—a former *moyel,* who was an expert with a knife—
stared at the man's fruit-filled sombrero. "Come again?"

"We want to hire you," Chiquita went on, trying to decide
if that had been an invitation.

"Sorry," Bris replied, quickly sizing him up. "We deal in
lead, not *lieder.*"

"That's what we want, you silly," Chiquita said, and then
informed him of the terrible conflict south of the border.
Chiquita also explained the situation in Mexico.

"I see," Bris replied. "What will you pay us?"

He showed him the sack of chocolates.

"*Nem zich a vaneh!*" Barnarish said with disdain.

"What does that mean?" asked Hernando.

"It means 'no,' with a little bit of 'lake' and 'jumping into' thrown in," Bris explained.

Chiquita frowned and removed the ring. He handed it to Bris, who called over a comrade. Harry Luchincop studied it with the loupe he carried for that purpose.

"Two carats . . . very white . . . internally flawless." Harry looked from Chiquita to Bris. "You, uh—gettin' hitched, boss?"

Bris faced Harry. "Clap."

"Huh?"

"Clap!"

Harry winked. "Don't worry. I won't say a word about the dose you got off that *kurveh* in Dodge—"

"Clap—your hands!" Bris snarled.

Harry did as he was told.

"Faster," Bris said.

Harry continued to clap. Chiquita started to dance El Jarabe Tapatio. As he swirled, his folklorico dress spun higher and higher above her legs.

"Oh," said Harry when he saw the other jewels Chiquita carried. "Never mind."

Bris agreed to help the Mexicans.

"You'd risk your life for non-Jews—and such low pay?" Harry asked.

"I once loved a non-Jew," Bris confessed. "A dance-hall girl."

"I didn't know that."

"Yes. I fell in love the moment I saw Gaza strip."

Harry looked at him, uncomprehending—and not quite sure he believed him.

The following morning, the gunmen met at the edge of Shlakberg. In addition to Bris, Harry, and Barnarish, there were Cheikuck, Leiden and Chris—who was the only non-Jew, having shortened from Christian to conceal that fact. The others teased that he was just .98 of a gunman, though he privately thought that with his foreskin he was technically more of a man than the rest.

The ride was hard and so was Chiquita. When they reached Nuevo Maízo, Señor Senior took him aside.

"Good news," the elder said.

"What?"

"We all know Jews have the horns," the elder told Chiquita, "so I sent all our young ladies to another village. You're now the best-looking piece in town."

Chiquita kissed the old man. Señor Senior wished he were wearing pants instead of a long-tailed Guayabera shirt. Then Chiquita might have kissed his weathered brow instead.

The Magnificent $5.98 set about making tactical improvements throughout Nuevo Maízo. They were nothing you could see, but when Halava rode into the village the following week he was surprised by fires that sprung from irrigation ditches. These were filled with burning oil, then driven back by an endless barrage of exploding kernels of corn.

When he left, the mood in the village was ebullient.

"Not only did we repel him," said one villager after helping to collect the projectiles, "but we have a delicious treat with which to celebrate!"

"Tasty but annoying," Bris said as he used a dirty fingernail to scrape pieces from between his teeth.

Their joy, however, was short lived. That night, while everyone slept, Halava and his men slipped back into town. They followed the trail of discarded dental floss to where Bris and the Jews were sleeping. The bandits then surrounded the Magnificent $5.98 and herded them into the neighboring desert.

"I'm not going to kill you," Halava told them. "I don't want a lawsuit. Also, you people have been known to come back from the dead. But I am keeping your horses and sending you home with just the food you were able to gather quickly before leaving."

With a throaty laugh Halava left the men to their fate after plucking the sack of gelt from Bris's saddlebag and keeping it for himself.

When he was gone, Bris spit.

"Only a fool would leave Jews in the desert with unleavened bread and tell them 'run,'" he said defiantly. "I'm going back."

"Are you a putz?" Harry Luchincop chided. "That village is full of goyim who hate us!"

"They'll hate us more if we leave," Bris suggested.

"Oh, right. Let me see," Harry tapped his chin, "since the Garden of Eden, who has been sorry to see Jews go?"

"Mama Buddha restaurant after they raised their prices," Bris said.

The men argued as though they were interpreting the Torah—for they were Jews first and saviors second. When all was done, if not said, they decided to return to the village. They had no choice. By then they had consumed all the matzo and would have starved, for gila monsters were not kosher.

It was just before dawn when the tired, hungry *nochshleppers* reached Nuevo Maízo. The village was still asleep, Halava and his men having partied well into the night.

"They'll need to dry out in the Cinquo de Mayo Clinic," observed Chris.

The Magnificent $5.98 ducked behind a stack of firewood.

"Lord God," said Bris, looking out at the rising sun, "before this day is done we will send Halava unto thee."

"Without nuts!" Barnarish vowed.

The Navajew swung his axe, causing the others to jump back. Bris tumbled against the firewood, knocking it over and rousing the dogs. They began to bark and the village began to stir.

"Damn, that porridge smells good," Harry Luchincop said as he sniffed what they were stirring.

But there was no time to think of breakfast. One of Halava's men had come over to tip a kidney in a pile of straw and saw the axe glinting in the sunrise.

Do You Feel Lucky, Boychick? The cunning, deadly Man with No Keepah—in this, the only known rendering of him—was the most feared Jewish gunslinger in the West. (A stone killer, he still used two sets of dishes on the frontier.)

My heroes have always been kosher cowboys. Among the earliest Jewish settlers in the Old West was Chaim Klepper, who founded the Bar Mitzvah Ranch in Nevada Territory. Here he is with his wife, Zissel. Klepper walked so slowly the locals started calling him Klepper the Schlepper.

My darling Clemenstein. Clementine "Clemmi" Clemenstein was one of the first Jewish saloon gals in the history of the American West. She captured the hearts of many men, from wealthy bankers and ranchers to desperados like Kid Goniff, the bankrobber, and Stuffy Derma, the cattle rustler. Clemmi ultimately retired from the saloon racket and opened the first kosher deli in the West, which featured delicacies like buffalo pastrami and stuffed breast of otter.

Borscht riders in the sky. Nathan "Nashville" Katz, had the distinction of being the first Jewish crooning cowboy. Some of his best-remembered hits include "Back in the Sable Again" and "(I Got Spurs That) Jingle, Jangle, Jingle, and Such a Headache They Give Me, You Shouldn't Know."

Have gelt, will travel. "So what do we need with seven? I can get five for half the price." When the Jewish settlement of Nuevo Matzo was attacked by the Mexican bandit Halava, the residents were too cheap to hire seven professional gunslingers, figuring five was enough. It wasn't. Pictured here is Halava, right after he was captured and converted to Judaism because, he said, the food was better.

True greps. Rabbi Avram Wolf was one of the pioneers who braved the brutal hardships of helping settle the American frontier. He was also one of the first white men to make nice with the Indians, who gave him the name Spits When He Talks.

Bumbling Tumbleweeds. Sister Sara Canberra, pictured here sans habit, was a nun who had to cross the plains pursued by French Protestants. She was helped along by two moyels, Benny and Sol, who were searching for a wagon train of newborns to circumcise.

Go west, young Moon. Here's a baby picture of Henny Young Moon, who billed himself as "that rollicking, crazy punslinger of the Grossinga tribe of Indians" and the first stand-up comic to ever play the frontier circuit. His real name was Mendel Zuckerbrot and he was from the Bronx. "Let me tell you," Henny wrote in his memoirs years later, "some of those dives in mining towns were rough. There were times I had to threaten the audience with the barrel of a 44-40 if they didn't laugh."

From snow you can't make a cheesecake. Julius and Myra Bernstein, who settled in Whitefish Station, Montana, in 1878 and opened a dairy farm. When Flossie the cow peed on a fresh batch of cream cheese one day, Myra would have killed the animal on the spot if hadn't meant mixing meat and dairy.

Gunfight at the _Oy Vey_ corral. A very early photo taken of Jack Weiner, a.k.a. Little Big Mensch, who was separated from his pioneer parents and adopted by the Pawnee chief, Buck Stops Here.

Don't fence me in, you putz. The Comanche Indians who kidnapped Sara Mindel Shayna when she was a child soon had cause to regret it. As she matured, she became the bossiest squaw on the reservation, earning her the name Tumak Lanu Famisht—in English, She Who Drives Us Crazy.

"Jews in the woodpile!" he cried, frowning because that didn't sound quite right.

Bris used the delay to strike the bandit's head with a log.

"Siesta time!" he shouted as the Mexican hit the hay.

Just then, Chiquita wandered over and glared at the recumbent form.

"Oh, sure. 'Meet me at the haystack at dawn and . . .'" Chiquita gasped when he noticed Bris and the others. *"Madre de dios!* You came back!"

"Hush!" Bris cautioned as he handed Chiquita the log. "Come! Help us fight these *shtunks!*"

"You gave me wood," Chiquita cooed, raising it high. He also hoisted the log. *"Viva la Revolución!"*

Chiquita's cry woke Halava and the rest of his men. The bandits staggered to their feet as the Magnificent $5.98 attacked.

"The Jews are charging!" one of the thugs cried.

"What else is new?" Halava snarled.

The skirmish was violent but quick. The men of Shlakberg made the oppressors pay for their crimes—with interest.

"What else is new?" Halava asked as his men fell dead around him, shot or stabbed from places of concealment or bludgeoned by Chiquita, who hid the log under his dress. The gang leader himself perished last through an act of God.

"Killed by his own greed," Señor Senior remarked, gazing at the corpse, which was covered with ugly hives. "Who knew he had a chocolate allergy?"

Sadly, the Magnificent $5.98 did not come through the confrontation unscathed. Barnarish perished protecting what he thought were children but were actually midgets en route from Tiny Town, while Harry Luchincop picked up a boobytrapped peso. The coin was attached to a scorpion and he perished in Bris's arms.

"Tell me I wasn't a fool," the dying man said. "Tell me I came to save Jews!"

"You did," Bris lied. "The truth is, there are Golds in the hills."

"A *shtik naches*," he gasped with his last breath.

Bris tried to remove the peso from Harry's dead hand, to cover at least one of his eyes, but his grip was too tight.

"Marked down even further," Bris said when the remaining men had gathered.

While the people of Nuevo Maízo cleaned up their village and looked forward to a bright new future, the Magnificent $3.98 prepared to depart.

"We will never forget what you have given us," Señor Senior told the men.

"More graves to dig," complained Hernando.

"And many hours we must now spend churning butter for this so-called 'popcorn,'" Jose added.

"Don't forget new friends, like 'The Magnificent $9,'" Chiquita said, winking at Chris, who blushed and decided to stay.

Bris, Cheikuck, and Leiden bid the townspeople a heartfelt "*Shalom con Dios!*" then set out on fresh horses, courtesy of the former Halava gang.

"Well," Bris said, "I wonder what kind of adventure is out there for three amigos?"

But that is another tale for another time.

Dances with Wolf

Lieutenant John Dundrearies was sick of it all.

The cavalry officer was sick of war, sick of death, and definitely sick of being told he had to cut his full, whiskery sideburns.

"They're a fire hazard!" Major Farmboy snarled as embers from the lieutenant's pipe nearly set his face ablaze.

Fed up with ball and chain of command, Lieutenant Dundrearies rode out one brilliant morning with the intention of deserting the band of Marylanders with whom he'd enlisted. Followed by other disgruntled, hirsute troops, the men from Baltimore stumbled upon a regiment of Confederate soldiers who were preparing to attack the Union position. Having the high ground and the advantage of surprise—and made a little feral by the sight of the clean-shaven young Rebel faces—the lieutenant led a charge which routed the enemy.

As a reward for his gallantry, the lieutenant was summoned to General Salvo's headquarters and offered his choice of post. The young officer walked to a large map on the wall and studied the western frontier.

"I select Fort Zion," he said.

"The pillbox?"

Dundrearies had a blank look.

"Obviously, you've never met a JAP," the general went on. "Are you sure you want to go there?"

"Yes, sir," the lieutenant replied. "I've always wanted to see the canyon, those steep purple-colored cliffs, the great Virgin River."

"So it's seclusion you want?"

"That, and I yearn for beautiful peaks."

The general said nothing more, for he happened to need men at that fort. However, Fort Zion was not located near Zion Park as Lieutenant Dundrearies obviously imagined, but at a settlement on the other side of the Great Salt Lake. The whiskered officer wasn't going to live among the Mormons but among the Jews. Talk about disappointing scenery: Not only did they have just one wife each, but the women wore unflattering black wigs and long black dresses. The general shuddered.

Setting out with his horse Pancho, Lieutenant Dundrearies imagined meeting fine Indian maidens and taking several wives, while Pancho imagined fields of grain. After a fortnight's travel, during which he ate nothing but scrawny, greasy rodents, what he found astonished him. There were no natural wonders, only a broad expanse of dry dirt with withered tufts of grass and bleached rock populated by sand-colored chuckwallas. In the midst of this barren, hellish wilderness was a stockade about the size of a circus tent, without the canvas. Judging from the lack of odor, a circus probably had more horses, too. There were no birds, no flies; it was too hot for them. It was also too hot for whiskers, though the officer had no intention of shaving.

The gate was open and there was no one inside. The only structures were an unmanned observation tower, an empty corral, and a deserted barracks. There was a sun-yellowed note nailed to the door:

> *Went to Colorado. Back when there's something*
> *to kill other than time.*

"Well, Pancho," Dundrearies said dejectedly, "I guess we can forget about wild oats for either of us."

Climbing the ladder of the observation tower, the lieutenant scanned the horizon for any signs of habitation. To his surprise, there was a low-lying mesa with a small village thereupon. Leaving his gear behind and watering Pancho in the near-empty trough, Dundrearies rode out to investigate.

What he found was even more surprising than the deserted fort.

There were Jews, dozens of them. They were living in huts made of a brick called kugelstone in a settlement named

Oremkeit. It was founded a decade earlier by the followers of
Rabbi Avram Wolf who went West in search of an Indian tribe
that sounded too good to be true. He was never able to find
the Paiute and collect whatever they were paying. Weary, the
Wolf pack unpacked and decided to stay on the mesa.

The lieutenant didn't find that out right away, for the oc-
cupants looked at him with suspicion and ignored his ques-
tions. Their only comments were that he was tracking dust
all over the community, and it would have been nice if he'd
brought Danish. Could this be the "pillbox" General Salvo
had mentioned?

Finally, though, he was approached by a woman who was
unlike the others. She was blonde and smiling and not covered in hot black buffalo robes. Her calfskin bikini revealed
a waist that did not suggest a diet of linzer tarts.

"I'm Lieutenant John Dundrearies," he said. "You are—?"

"Stands With A Plug," she said.

"Unusual name," he said. "What does it mean? A rundown
horse? A bullet?"

She did not answer. "Soldiers do not often come here."

"That's a shame," he said as he watched several Jews
dancing in a circle. "Soldiers like cheap *horas*."

"These people are suspicious of everyone, even each
other," she said. "They only let you in because, from a distance, they thought your sideburns were *payes*."

Dundrearies looked around. "There are no fences. No one
wears a gun. How would they have kept me out?"

"They rely on a powerful medicine," she replied. "They sneer in a way that is most ugly. Sometimes they narrow and avert their eyes, spit through their fingers, and mutter in a strange, guttural tongue."

"Are those 'JAPs'" he asked.

"No," she replied. "The JAP medicine is even more powerful. It is spoken scorn."

"You are not one of them," Dundrearies observed.

"I am a *shiksa*," she explained. "I like sex, and I do not give my opinion unless asked, and then politely."

"Why are you here?"

"I am originally from Atlanta. They took me in. I was stoned."

"Why those Old Testament rapscallions!" Dundrearies reached for his sidearm. "Why did they do that?"

"No, I mean I was high," she said. "I'd been traveling west with my family. We were starving, and I ate strange toadstools. That night, I was so dizzy I fell from the wagon. No one heard me. The next morning, a Hebrew saw my hair gleaming on the prairie and, thinking it was gold, came and got me. He had to carry me. I was so wrecked."

"Didn't your family come back for you?"

"When they heard I was found by a Jewish man, they wrote back thanking the Lord that I would be well taken care of."

Dundrearies holstered his weapon, and the young blonde took him to the tent of her savior, a doctor named Kochedik

Bird. Because he was not allowed to marry outside the faith, Stands With A Plug stayed with him as a nurse.

"What do you do?" the lieutenant asked her.

"I insert the herbal suppositories," she explained.

That explained the name, Dundrearies thought. "So tell me—what kind of ailments would require such a treatment, for on the way to Fort Zion, I supped often on prairie dog and now feel disquiet in my bowels—"

"I will give you a buffalo milk enema," Kochedik Bird told him.

"—which I expect will pass," Dundrearies added.

The woman—whom he learned was considered a "Jew-tile," an adopted gentile who was able to enunciate Yiddish without embarrassing herself—showed Dundrearies around the settlement, introducing him to the chief, Never Buys Retail, and explaining the white strings that many of the young men wore around their belts.

"It is called 'Jewish scalping,' wearing the tsitsis or tassels of those whom they have vanquished," she explained.

"These people make war among themselves?"

"*Bist meshuggeh?*" she asked. "What war? Whoever earns the most takes the fringe from he who earns the least."

"So strife among the Jews is fought with tiny shears and money?"

She shook her long blonde locks. "With that and also words, insults, and sometimes long periods of not talking to someone, often for a generation or more. This is different from revenge, which is accomplished by amassing profit at the expense of another."

It was a world Lieutenant Dundrearies had never known existed. After too many years of soldiering and disciplinary actions over facial hair, he was among people to whom both of these quantities were alien. He thought of the whirling Jews he had seen earlier.

"I should very much like to remain here," he told her.

"First you must learn to dance with Wolfs," she told him. "And to do that, you must first earn their trust."

"How?"

"A test, and . . ." She rubbed her thumb against her first two fingers.

Lieutenant Dundrearies understood. He requested an audience with Rabbi Wolf, which was granted. The patriarch lived under a chuppah, which he explained was a canopy for performing weddings.

"Why take it down and have to store it, *shlep* it, and put it up again?" the rebbe asked. "Plus, I get a very nice breeze."

He looked Dundrearies over. In addition to his *payes*, the cavalry officer wore a buckskin jacket with fringe and a head covering with decorative sabers in front.

"Gold?" the rabbi asked, raising a spindly finger at the crossed swords.

"Brass, sir," the lieutenant replied.

The rabbi frowned. "Can you say *tuchas*?"

Having been briefed by Stands With A Plug, Dundrearies

enunciated the word as though he were saying "to us" clearing his throat.

"Not bad," the rabbi said. Then his hand fell open, palm up.

Dundrearies regarded it. Then, slowly, he placed his own hand on top and shook hard.

"Stands With A Plug told me I should give you something valuable," he replied. "So I give you my friendship."

The rabbi's frown deepened. "The Torah would say that I should accept this gift . . . but I will also take the horse, which you can rent back from me."

Since he wanted to remain in the settlement—and in particular get to know the healing touch of Stands With A Plug—Dundrearies agreed.

After being permitted to join the reeling *hora* circle—but only for a half-turn, for he threw up his hands like he was hoisting baled hay and tossed the *chazentah* on her face, earning him the title Dances Like A *Yukel*—Dundrearies returned to the fort to gather his gear. There, to his horror, the lieutenant discovered that not only had the soldiers returned, they were planning to visit Oremkeit.

"We run outta pay," Sergeant Preplen said to the new arrival. "So's we figgered t'go tuh the Jews and git some."

"But—the interest they charge!" Dundrearies said. "Why not just wait for payday?"

"We'll go off our nuts here, sir," he replied. "Besides, I think we can get the Hebrews to make a donation!" the sergeant laughed, drawing his saber.

The lieutenant knew the Jews would never agree. Turning Pancho around, Dundrearies rode back to the mesa and told Rabbi Wolf what was afoot.

"I've been expecting this day," he sighed and called over to the treasurer. "Irving?"

"I'm counting!"

"You still have that chest of Confederate money?"

"I've been giving it to the children to play Savings and Loan."

"Let's give it to those *onshikenishes* from the fort," the rabbi said. "By the time they find out what it is, we'll be on the road."

"You'd leave Oremkeit?" Dundrearies asked.

"Why not?" the rabbi asked, shrugging his small shoulders. "Besides, it's time we finished our search for the Paiute."

"But rabbi, I don't think you'll find what you're looking for."

"*Nar ainer!*" the patriarch chuckled. "No Jew ever does! That's why we keep looking! Send the rental for the horse in care of Ida Newman in northwest Baltimore," the rabbi added. "She'll make sure I get it."

The lieutenant nodded and turned to Stands With A Plug. "What about you?" Dundrearies asked. "Will you go with them or come back to the fort with me?"

"Do they have bacon?"

"By the crateful."

"Let's go," she said, and they rode off, the Confederate chest in a cart and the blonde's chest pressed against his back.

Dundrearies smiled. He had not found the peaks he sought, but these would do.

Two Moyels for Sister Sara

Legend has it that six score years ago, Sara Canberra was on her way to Australia when she got sidetracked—by God.

She left Ohio, stopped in a church in Colorado to rest, and instead of crossing the ocean to search for gold found an epiphany. Leaving the cake-box building, she made her way toward Mexico to pursue a different cause.

That was what put her on the Gila River with the Krazimatzo Brothers on that fateful morning.

The young beauty had stopped to wash away the clinging filth of travel when three men showed up to do the same: wash the filth from her.

"Would you please go elsewhere?" she asked, for she was knee-deep in the waters and her clothing lay in a pile back on the bank.

"But this is our favorite spot . . . now," snickered one of the brothers.

The second brother nodded stupidly while the third just stared at her ass, a handsome gray African donkey.

Suddenly, a voice cracked from behind the gang.

"Step away from *di maidel*."

The brothers turned. They saw two figures standing atop a buckboard, their long black dusters hanging to below the knees. The pair had on flat-brimmed black hats pulled low and held small knives by the tips, ready to throw.

"What's a *temaidel*?" asked one of the brothers.

"He said 'tomato,'" said another looking around for the offending salad ingredient.

"Stop talking and start shooting!" yelled the third brother.

The men reached for their guns but never got to fire. While their backs were turned, the woman had picked up a 7-pound trout and proceeded to hit them hard against the back of the neck. The three went down like sacks of meal.

"A regular Esther," said the taller of the men in *shvartze*.

"Williams?" said the other.

"No, Benji, not Esther Williams. Queen Esther. From Purim."

The woman hurried to gather her clothing as the two new arrivals turned their backs.

"I am Saul and this is my brother Benjamin," said the older of the two.

"I am Sara," the woman said as she dressed.

"I got shmutz on my blade," moaned Benji as he inspected his scalpel.

"We'll clean them both before we reach Shlakberg," said Saul.

The woman perked. "You're going south?"

"Like *tantes* in winter," said Benji.

"Could you possibly escort me to Mexico?"

"For free?" Saul asked.

"I can pay you when we reach the church in Tijuana."

"Church?" Saul turned. He dropped his blade when he saw the woman. "*Gevald!* You're a nun!"

"She's a Hebrew letter?" Benji asked.

"No!" said Saul. He picked up the scalpel and spit on it. "She's an *uber-shiksa!*" He wiped off his wet tool and ran back to the buckboard.

The other man looked at the woman in her habit. "We can't just leave her. When these men wake up, they'll go after her."

Saul picked up the reins. "That is related to the removal of the prepuce how?"

"This woman is married to the Lord," Benji said ominously.

"Different godhead," Saul said. He sat in thought, as though he was trying to remember what Hebrew year it was. The woman did swing a powerful trout. Maybe she could protect them. "*Tsum glik, tsum shlimazel,*" he said. "We will all go."

So it came to pass that Sara joined the two men, attaching her own animal and mule cart to the back of the buckboard and sitting between them on the seat for warmth. It was early December, and the sun was setting, and her body was still wet from the river. She learned that the brothers were both *moyels*. Saul was the older and more experienced while Benji was just learning his trade.

"What made you want to do such work?" she asked.

"Jewish heredity," replied Saul.

"Tradition?"

"No, our mother insisted," he told her. "I wanted to write klezmer songs."

"And I wanted to be a gynecologist," Benji said.

"But she wanted us to honor the word of God," Saul explained.

"You mean, do what she told you to do?"

"No, the other God," Benji replied. "The one who ordered that Jewish males be circumcised."

"Ah. That must be very challenging work," Sara remarked, trying to find something positive to say.

Saul shrugged. "It's like trimming the raw crust from pies, only it's *shmeckel*."

"Have you ever seen one?" Benji asked, as he helpfully reached to undo his trousers for her benefit.

"Yes, on a horse," she answered.

Benji left his pants on, and they rode several miles in silence. Just before sunset, they stopped and made camp. The earth here was dry and barren, but at least it was flat. Benji used a wooden menorah taper to light the fire.

"Do you have a ceremony to perform on this trip, or do you roam the West looking for foreskins?" Sara asked.

"Four," Saul replied as he honed the blades.

"For what?" Sara said.

"Foreskins," Saul replied. "We have four to do."

"You travel for four foreskins."

"That's right," Saul told her. "We're always very busy this time of year. Tax-deduction babies."

They broke camp early the next morning, Benji making sure that Sara's belongings were secure.

"So, sister, what's in those trunks you're carrying?" Benji asked. He chuckled. "Changes of clothes?"

"Dynamite," she replied easily.

Saul spit out the sunflower seeds he'd been chewing, and Benji started running.

"*Steitsh!*" Saul cried. "Why is a woman of God carrying TNT?"

"I'm on a holy mission," she replied. "French soldiers in Tijuana kidnaped my sister. I intend to save her and destroy their garrison."

Benji stopped. "Wait . . . you want to blow up the French?"

"Yes. "

"Oh. Okay."

"Hold on," Saul said. "When you say 'my sister,' do you mean a nun or your sibling?"

"My sister sister," said Sara. "She was studying to become a nun."

Saul thought for a moment. "Tijuana is not far. If we hurry, we can go there and help you free your sister sister sister and still be in Shlaksberg for the *bris*."

"My brother, if we help save a *shiksa* is that a *mitzvah* or a sin?" Benji asked.

"That's a very good question," Saul answered. "We will find out on Yom Kippur."

Going as fast as the rutted road and trunks filled with dynamite would allow, the two moyels and Sister Sara traveled until they crossed the border and the scent of beans and tortillas filled their nostrils. They pushed on until that smell was supplanted by the pungent odor of *brochettes de crevettes*. The only time they stopped was so Benji could make sure the crates were secure in the wagon.

Throughout the journey, Benji was deep in thought. "You know, there's something a *bisel* strange about all of this," he whispered to his brother as they neared the French garrison in Tijuana.

"Just a *bisel*?" Saul snickered. He was still pondering Benji's earlier observation.

"The Krazimatzo brothers are Jewish, yet they did not understand Yiddish," Benji remarked.

"Maybe they've taken too many knocks on the head," Saul said.

"Or maybe we were meant to find them and Sara," Benji went on.

"Why?"

"They are well-known criminals," Benji said, "and such cargo as this would have been confiscated at the border by the *Federales*. Yet no one bothered inspecting the wagons of two *moyels* and a nun."

"It's possible," Saul agreed. "Perhaps the Krazimatzo brothers hate the French, too."

"Or perhaps we're not going to attack the French," Sister Sara said from behind a pistol. "You two are such—how do you say it? *Mummers?*"

Benji winced. "*Mamzers.*"

Saul smacked him. "Don't help her insult us, *yutz!*"

"Mr. Bal Torah, '*Mummers*' is worse," Benji insisted.

"Be quiet!" Sara ordered as the Krazimatzo brothers rode over a rise. The three grizzled robbers stopped at her side. The nearest gave her a kiss on the mouth.

Benji poked his brother, "See? I was right!"

"I'm *kvelling*," Saul moaned.

"God isn't going to like his wife kissing a bandit," Benji added.

"Shmuck, she isn't a nun!"

"She's not?"

"That's right," Sara said, her cheek red with beard burn. "I met the brothers at church—when they were robbing it. They told me about a bank in Tijuana that held the French payroll. We came up with a plan to get the dynamite here."

"*Trombenik!*" Benji blurted and doubled over. "I need to lie down."

Saul helped him to the mule cart while Sara doffed her habit. He leaned against the crates, hyperventilating.

"What're we gonna do with these *shmendricks?*" the kissing brother asked.

"They're harmless," she said. "Let's tie them up and leave them here. We'll be in and out of Tijuana before they can notify—"

"I don't think so!" Benji sang out. In one hand he held a stick of dynamite. In the other was a menorah taper.

"A *kramp in di kishkes!*" one of the brothers cried. "He wasn't really sick!"

"You were right, Benji," Saul admitted. "They may not be too smart, but they do understand Yiddish."

"Okay, you *mieskeits,*" Benji said, striking the wick against the rough side of the mule cart. "You've got until the wick burns my fingers to leave the money you took from the church and ride away."

"He's bluffing," Sara cried. "He'll blow up, too!"

"Not if we're going the other direction," Saul said as he mounted the seat of the buckboard.

"And I can throw like a Koufax," Benji warned.

It took another moment for the gang leader to throw down his saddlebags. Then he and the other men rode south. Sara stayed where she was.

"Let's make a deal," she said. "We can take the bank without the Krazimatzo brothers. We'll split the French money."

"We're not *gonefs*," Saul said. "We want bargains, not crooked deals."

With a huff, Sara unhitched her donkey and followed the Krazimatzos.

The brothers carefully loaded the crates into the buckboard. *"G'ya Mogen, g'ya Clamp,"* he cried as he guided the horses north.

"Are we really going to return the money to the church?" Benji asked.

"The minute we are through in Shlaksberg," Saul told him.

"God may spare us, but when mama hears this she will give us each a *zetz*," Benji sighed.

"Maybe not. We'll sell the dynamite in Shlaksberg and buy her something nice."

"Why not just give her the dynamite?" Benji suggested. "She always wants to light a fuse under someone's *tuchas*."

Saul did not explain why that was a bad idea. Instead, he sat back, hummed a klezmer melody that still lacked words, and marveled—as they passed their old camp late in the day—how between sunrise and sunset the spit seedlings had turned overnight to sunflowers. . . .

Henny Young Moon, Indian Comedian

It was called *Pupiklech* Sage because it lined the *Pupiklech* Trail which carried *Pupiklech* comedians from Chicago to San Francisco starting in the late 1880s. The funnymen got the name—which they gave to the trail and its environs—from the diet of chicken gizzards on which they survived. That was the only part of the chicken they could beg or buy from local farmers, tavern-owners, and travelers they met at campsites.

Henny Young Moon was a member of the Grossinga tribe, a small band of river dwellers who lived a half-day's ride from the trail. One afternoon in 1875, a young brave was unsuccessfully trying to spear a freshwater fish. When at last he succeeded, he proudly showed the wriggling catch to his father.

"*Carp die-um*," he cried, which amused a Catholic missionary so much that the clergyman wet himself most unbecomingly.

Realizing that comedy was stronger medicine than arrows, the tribe began to sharpen their wit instead of their spearheads.

The Grossingas were all but wiped out by the 7th Cavalry that same year at a spot known as Wounded Funnybone.

"It is not right that comedians should die," said an angry young Henny Young Moon as he surveyed the carnage. The youthful Grossinga had escaped destruction because he was coincidentally dressed as a squaw while rehearsing an Uncas Miltie routine.

Alone and wearing an antelope-skin skirt and matching blouse, which was padded with buffalo hump, Henny was taken to a reservation where he learned English, so that he could slay the White Man as well as his own people. When he was ready, he escaped by distracting the sentry with a joke.

"Did you hear about the guard who heard a noise, fired, then shouted, 'Who went there?'" Henny asked.

As the young soldier grappled with the punch line, Henny slipped through the gate and made his way to the Pupiklech Trail where he happened to meet up with a covered wagon overfilled with comedians from the East.

"We go West, young man!" one of them quipped.

"I am Young Moon," Henny corrected him, "and I know the territory. If you take me along, I can guide you."

"How," said one of the men.

"I'll draw a map," Henny replied.

"That was a joke," Ramrod Dangerfield explained.

The group made room for Henny by tossing Dangerfield from the wagon. He had never experienced such disrespect.

There were not very many Indian comics at this time. As Henny himself explained it while touring with the Eastern comedians, "Native peoples don't have a lot to laugh about. With the buffalo nearly gone, the only way we get to eat is with reservations."

Audiences of all kinds laughed at his humor, and at his Indian dress—the same one he had worn when escaping the massacre. As the conservative humor critic Rush Hashana wrote in his column, "In the end, Henny Young Moon knows what the audience wants. He is also a realist. He acknowledges that his people simply got stuck on the wrong side: geno."

Rave reviews of Henny's act preceded him by wire, resulting in sold-out gigs along the Pupiklech Trail. Then, suddenly, audiences began to thin as word reached him of an even greater comedian, one who was drawing larger crowds with something called shtick. He was the Jewish comedian William Katz, who went by the stage name Billy the Kidder. As Henny discovered, telegrams were fast. But tell-a-grandma or any other Jew and word spread as if by magic. Billy was so successful that he didn't travel slowly by land, like the others, but by river and sea aboard a fancy vessel custom made in El Dorado, a "Jew Boat."

There were some who said his humor was mediocre, and he got laughs by threatening audiences with the barrel of a

44-40. Even the posters suggested as much, indicating that he was "a comic of high caliber." But none of that mattered. Gunslinger or punslinger, whether people came to laugh or to see hecklers shout, he was drawing crowds.

One hot summer night, it so happened that both Henny and Billy were appearing not far from one another in California: Billy at the famed Segundo City and Henny at the less-renowned Improvident.

Because Billy did only one show, he was able to catch Henny's second set. He sat in the back of the club, his Borsalino black hat pulled low, his dark eyes alert. There was a bottle of seltzer on the table, and he carried just two items: a tallis bag with a gold "BK" on the outside and a Winchester revolver inside; and a gold Torah pointer he used to brush flies from his drink, a Shirley Temple Beth El.

A not-so-young woman with painted cheeks and also painted cheekbones sidled up to the table.

"Where're you from, good lookin'?" she asked.

"Honolulu."

"Hawaii?"

"Fine, thanks," he told her.

The woman was confused but undaunted. "Mind if I join you?"

"Why, am I coming apart?"

The *gesunteh moid* half-smiled. "I get it. A comedian."

"Actually, I am," Billy replied. "But I save the good stuff for paying customers."

"So do I," she winked.

He looked at her torn dress with her *tuchas* hanging out. "You might want to freshen the billboard. It doesn't seem to be attracting any business."

With a snarl, the woman stormed away, paint chips falling like glitter. As an afterthought, she broke wind hard in his direction.

Though grateful for the blast that drew the flies away like a formation of geese, Billy swatted the departing hussy with his Torah pointer.

She turned angrily. "Who do you think you are?" she yelled and glanced at the bag. "What's that stand for, Big *K'nocker*?"

"Nope," he drawled, slowly raising his tallis bag and pointing it at the oncoming *nafkeh*. "Billy the Kidder."

The woman stopped on a dime. Not being Jewish, she left it on the floor. "So—is that a gun in your bag or is this a Bar Mitzvah?"

Billy grinned. "That's almost funny."

"How about we start all over?" she asked. "I'll put your initials on my cheeks for a very reasonable rate."

"Thanks," he said, "but all people will see is Abraham Lincoln in the middle."

The woman flushed with rage as the footlights were turned on, and Henny was introducced by the proprietor, Bubee Friedman.

"Now, the man who'll heat a scalp to make your wigwam— Henny Young Moon!"

"Welcome," Henny said as he stepped onto the stage. "You may have noticed I'm dressed like a squaw. Been doing it ever since my wife found Minnehaha's clothes in our teepee and demanded an explanation.

"But seriously, my wife only married me because she misunderstood when I said I had a lodge pole. . . ."

The more Billy listened, the angrier he became.

"My wife sent me out for three skins, but I came back with fore," Henny said, "and boy, were those pony soldiers sore. . . .

"Too much chamomile will make your teepee. . . .

"How do you like my sense of Yuma . . . ?"

This isn't humor, Billy thought. There were no witty observations or devastating insights, just plays on words and stereotypes.

In other words, their acts were identical. Henny Young Moon had to be stopped before he became a serious rival.

After the show, Billy stuffed the Torah pointer in his belt, took something from the table, then went to the stage door and waited. He held the *tallis* bag in his left hand, his finger anxiously rubbing the velvet. He also had a challah knife in his right boot. Billy was ready to end this rivalry.

A few fans gathered in the alley. When Henny emerged, he graciously accepted their drunken applause and assumed the vomiting was just gurgled cheers. Billy walked up to the Grossinga and, without warning, hit him full in the face with a shot from the seltzer bottle he'd taken from the table.

But, as usual, Henny was not unprepared. He swung a bottle of carbonated water from behind his back. It struck Billy in the shoulder. The tallis bag fell to the mud and the seltzer dropped, *shpritzing* mud and regurgitated nachos on five pairs of shoes.

"How do you like my club soda?" Henny hooted as seltzer water ran down his own dark face.

The men in the alley oooohed at the gag.

"I'd call this showdown a wash," Billy replied.

The men in the alley aaaahed.

"*Wasser* up?" the *gesunteh moid* quipped as she sashayed from the club behind Henny.

"Mensa-mensa," the men in the alley agreed, moving their hands from side to side.

"Thanks for the warning—and the Schweppes," Henny said to her.

"It was a pleasure," she sneered.

"So, it took two of you to defeat me," Billy laughed, then regarded Henny. "How do you think you'd do one on one?"

"Just jokes?" the Indian asked, glancing at the fallen *tallis* bag.

"Sure, assuming you actually know any," Billy replied.

That was all Henny could stands 'cause he can't stands no more. "Let's go," said the Indian, and walked toward the street.

The men stopped in the middle of the dark, empty thoroughfare. The evening wind blew hard and loud off the Bay, carrying crumpled paper and discarded scraps of food. It sounded and felt just like a weekday night at the club.

They were standing forty paces from one another. The crowd from the alley joined them, along with patrons from the other clubs and saloons. The object of the duel was simple. The first participant to laugh at his opponent's joke was the loser.

"My lawyer is a genius," Billy said, warming up. "He can tell at a glance whether a contract is oral or written."

The crowd tittered. Henny was implacable.

"My lawyer practices in Buffalo," Henny shot back. "His wife is big and hairy."

The crowd made a *ewww* sound, but there were some chuckles. Billy's face remained impassive.

The two men stepped closer.

"One day, Alcatraz will have a pen that works on water."

"My doctor enjoys bad health."

"My tribal shaman knows his medicine, man."

"My wife's a carpenter. You oughta see her build."

"My brother married an Oto. He doesn't know whether he's coming or going."

The gags flew, the men moving a step closer after each round. Neither of them smiled during the exchange. When they were nose to nose, only one joke each remained.

"The baby couldn't decide whether he wanted bottle or bust," Billy said.

Henny felt his mouth twitch, but held on. "An Apache fell down a cliff while speaking sign language," Henny said. "He screamed his hands off."

Billy's eyes opened wide and he chortled. He swallowed it quickly but it was too late.

"You laughed!" shouted the *gesunteh moid*. "Henny is the winner!"

Billy's eyes narrowed angrily, and he thrust a hand into his boot. He drew the challah knife and lunged at Henny. Fortunately, the blade did not draw blood for Henny was still wearing his dress and the knife struck his buffalo mound bosom.

"Busted!" Billy cried as Henny whipped the Torah pointer from his opponent's belt and struck him with it repeatedly.

The crowd cheered as the sore loser went down. However, many also laughed at what would have been the winning joke had Billy said it earlier. Even Henny chuckled. In life, as in comedy, timing is everything.

Henny stopped the pummeling after a few moments and gazed at his fallen foe. "I won. And I've beaten you."

The crowd laughed even louder.

Henny drew the knife from his breast. "That should've raised a titter," he said.

The crowd laughed harder still. The Grossinga's foe was utterly beaten.

"But it's wrong to fight like this," the Indian continued. "There is enough room for everyone."

With that, Henny Young Moon helped William Katz to his feet, and the two went off with the *gesunteh moid* to share a few drinks and tell a few jokes. Henny actually learned a great deal from the veteran comedian, whose shtick is remembered even today as the Katz skills.

The Wild Brunch

Whitefish Station, Montana, was known for its scenic beauty, clean air, and, of course, its whitefish, including lake herring. There was no better freshwater catch this side of the Ukraine, and it was one of the reasons Myra and Julius Bernstein moved from Erie, New York. Julius had made his fortune providing oar poles for barges plying the Erie Canal. He moved West, rather hastily, when diplomats from Warsaw came looking for them. The Bernsteins wanted to be where the countryside was open, where the fish was fresh, and where the federal government had limited jurisdiction.

Cut off from friends and family back East, the Bernsteins held a monthly brunch at their dairy farm to which every member of the local community was invited. This time, though, it was a special gathering: the rebbe and rebbetzen from Butte were coming, not just to *fress* but to take orders for the beautiful copper *tchatchkes* their son the jeweler was making.

In addition, Julius's younger brother had written of his intentions to join the gathering. The good news was that he had given up trying to find gold in California. The bad news was that he had become something called a Jew for Jesus.

"What is that?" Myra moaned when she read the passage.

"If it's not a Mexican politician, we may have tsuris," Julius replied.

But that was not the worst of it. Myra had gone out to check the ice tub—a cedar vat lined with sheet metal on top of rabbit fur for insulation. It was filled with ice from the river and was used to keep the newly made cream cheese cold. Unfortunately, Flossie the cow had peed on the tub, warming it and causing the ice to melt and the cream cheese to spoil. Myra would have slain the animal on the spot, except it would have mixed meat and dairy.

"What will we give our guests to put on their bagels?" she wailed.

"Don't we have butter?"

"For the goyim, yes," she said. "Are you going to send someone or should I go all the way to town myself?"

Julius dispatched his quickest rider, Johnny Tov, to Billings for cream cheese. Julius had always liked the name of that town. Johnny returned just as the first guests were arriving. He handed Myra a bucket. She sniffed disapprovingly.

"What's this?" she asked.

"All the general store had was garlic cream cheese," he said.

"Those Livorno Jews!" she shook a fist.

"Ma'am, I also went to the camp of the Chinese railroad workers," Johnny said as he handed her a second pail. "They use soy beans to make a product they call 'I Can't Believe It's Not Shmear.' I got that too."

Myra seemed happier with this and, adding chives, hoped the Jews wouldn't know the difference. She set both on the table.

Shopkeepers and ranch hands, the schoolteacher and the telegraph operator, even local clergy of other faiths came for the celebrated buffet. The arrival of the rabbi made the day especially memorable, as he rarely went to dairy farms. Being anywhere near "curds" made the Middle East native anxious.

And then a dry, sandy cloud appeared on the horizon. Julius looked up from his chopped liver. As the rider neared, he saw that it was his brother Melvin. He'd been hoping the *shmegegi* had stopped at the saloon, as usual, and stayed there.

"Y'shua!" the young man cried as he neared.

"Gesundheit!" Julius said hopefully.

The rabbi tapped him on the shoulder. "Y'shua is the Hebrew name for Jesus."

"In that case, *gevald*," Julius replied, slapping an open palm to his forehead.

"And it looks like he came empty-handed," the rabbi added as he bit into his fourth macaroon.

Melvin swung from the saddle before his horse had fully

stopped, causing him to stumble into a card table. He knocked the cheese plate and a bowl of macaroni salad into the lap of the local grocer. A dog licked it off eagerly, causing Mr. Kraft to wonder if people might like the combination as well.

"Good news!" Melvin cried after regaining his balance.

"You're earning a living?" Julius asked.

"Not that kind of good news!" Melvin laughed. "We can all be saved by receiving God's free gift of salvation in His Son, the Messiah!"

"That is no gift," the rabbi snorted. "You have to put money in the plate to get their God's blessings."

"What is money but the tool of vice and oppression?" he asked.

"Then you're not earning a living," Julius sighed.

"He's not even a Jew!" the rabbi cried.

"He sounds like a Marxist," Johnny Tov remarked.

"Actually, where the Gospels are concerned, I'm more of a Lukist," Melvin informed him.

A confused silence fell upon the spread. It was broken when the rebbetzen took a bite of her bagel.

"What's this?" she said, her lips smacking noisily and unhappily as she chewed.

"It's a cinnamon bagel," Myra said, adding quickly, "try some lox on it—"

"No," the woman continued, her tongue unfolding like a tsunami of flesh, also carpeted with white. "What's on the bagel?"

"Chives."

"Which are in . . . ?"

The silence deepened.

"Chinks," the hostess replied, her voice softer than tumbling tumbleweeds.

"You're serving 'I Can't Believe It's Not Shmear'?" the rabbi's wife cried with jowl-rattling horror.

The hostess nodded timidly. Much less timidly, her guest sought a napkin into which she could deposit the offending load.

"She always spits," the rabbi sighed.

Melvin offered the woman his kerchief and an aphorism. "Y'shua said, 'I am the living bread that came down from heaven. Whoever eats of this bread will live forever.'"

The woman not only surrendered a mouthful, she made the *shpayen* on Melvin.

"Her ladyship is a rabbi's wife!" Johnny Tov yelled. "You don't go yappin' all 'bout Jesus!"

"But Y'shua is the light—"

"Y'sure?" quipped Freddie "Roamin' " Sikes, the village *shmendrick*.

"He's sure," said a man who had ridden up, dark and silent, during the debate.

"Bishop Pike!" ejaculated the rabbi as his wife spit again. "What are you doing here?"

"He has a standing invitation," Julius said sheepishly.

"Then let him stand over there," the rabbi motioned toward the house.

The clergyman dismounted and strode forward. He stood

a head higher than the rabbi, and he didn't have a wife. That made him stand even taller. His spurs were tiny crosses. "I stand with the Lord," Pike said.

"God is on the porch," the rabbi said. "I see Him. Look! Go and have a talk with him there."

"Y'shua is everywhere!" Melvin pointed out.

The priest was unconvinced. He seemed to be looking for Him between the rabbi's eyes. Julius inserted himself between the men.

"Let's eat," he said, handing the priest a cherry danish and leading him away.

"Try the cream cheese, *dershtikt zolstu veren!*" the rebbetzen shouted after him.

Melvin frowned. "That's not very nice, telling him to choke on it."

"Why not?" the rabbi asked. "Then Y'shua can bring him back like Lazarus!"

"Why are you being so rude?" Melvin asked.

"That man once called me a cheap Jew."

"I said chief!" the priest shouted over his shoulder. "I was explaining your job to a Cheyenne!"

"You were telling him why I wouldn't buy his blankets," the rabbi replied. "You said Jews weren't as tall as Christians."

"I said Jews wore a tallis, unlike Christians!"

The rabbi shrugged dismissively. "That's not what I heard."

The priest had had enough. He flung the pastry at his fellow clergyman. The danish hit him in the forehead with a splat, sending a long lash of cherry filling over his head and soiling his *keepah.*

"*Nisht gut,*" Myra gasped as she hurried over with a napkin.

Meanwhile, Johnny Tov responded by flipping a jam-covered bagel as though he were skipping a flat stone. It slashed against the priest's chest, dying his black vestments red, the ooze dripping onto his boots.

Unable to contain himself, Melvin jumped at Tov. As he did, he upset a bowl of shrimp dip on a nearby table. The sauce cascaded through the air, splashing onlookers with spicy red streams and droplets. The guests jumped back, screaming as it stained their clothes and stung their eyes.

Off to one side the rabbi and the priest were dripping with red and circling one another warily, like Pat Garrett and Billy the Kid. The priest held a cross of iron, the rabbi was just looking to get away.

The Bernsteins were oy-oy-oying as they watched the *fracas,* running here and there to keep the others from taking sides, though accepting a few side bets as to whether Melvin or Johnny Tov would come out on top.

Order was only restored when a local dramatist went to one of the tables and began tossing red herrings at the combatants. Unable to concentrate on their adversaries, they gave up the struggle.

The carnage was absolute. Linen was flecked with mud

and preserves. Frightened horses nudged carts in front of them for protection. Sausage and cottage cheese lay together unnaturally.

Melvin had turned the other cheek and been knocked silly by Johnny Tov. He rose unsteadily and turned his two shiners toward his assailant.

"I forgive you," Melvin said.

Tov offered him a hand. "I accept your helping of black-eyed peace."

The priest regarded the rabbi.

"We appear to be at a crossroads," the churchman said.

"You got a less goyisha word for where we are?" the rabbi challenged, covertly squeezing bialys to find the stalest one, in case he was forced to throw it.

"We have a choice," the priest said, his tone conciliatory. "To fight or not."

Hidden by her sprawling *tuchas*, the rebbetzen passed her husband a large carrot stick.

"I suggest," the priest went on, "that whichever of us is without sin should cast the first stone." He produced, from behind his own back, his own fist-sized rock. He tossed it up and down threateningly.

The rabbi twirled his beard thoughtfully. "Where'd that come from? I didn't see you bend."

"God delivered it to me."

"It was on the table, holding down the napkins," Julius whispered.

The rabbi sighed his resignation then turned to his wife. "What was I supposed to do with this?" he asked, shaking the vegetable at her.

"What does anyone do with a carrot?" she asked. "You should fight on an empty stomach?"

With peace restored, Johnny Tov hauled over buckets of water while the group picked up those food items which could be cleaned and eaten, such as apples and tomatoes. Meanwhile, Myra got fresh cold cuts from the chickens and cows. She hadn't planned on butchering them so soon, but a Jewish woman is always prepared for slaughter.

As late afternoon surrendered to dusk, Julius addressed the gathering.

"Same day next month?" he asked.

"That's Easter," the priest pointed out as he chewed on a large, juicy strawberry—and eyed the rabbi warily.

"So?" said the rabbi, testing the heft of a tomato as he pretended to study it. "Why should the rest of us suffer?"

"Hosanna!" cried Melvin. "We are at last united for we cannot forget the great rabbi who suffered that day at the hands of other Jews!"

Melvin was instantly pelted with fruit. He contorted slowly, first to the left, then to the right, then arching and tumbling to the ground. Streaks of red erupted from the impact, leaving him sprawled in a sea of scarlet pulp.

The group skipped brunch the following month, and it is said that the soil of Whitefish retains the crimson scars of that fateful day. No one was untouched by the violence, not even Myra and Julius's young son Peter, whose pet rooster had been sacrificed to feed the multitude.

As he sobbed to his father in what was to prove the final comment on the violent day, "I am sad there won't be no more peckin', paw."

Little Big Mensch

J wasn't looking for a conversation when I went to the park. Only a bit of sun and quiet in which to read my copy of *Decisive Battles of the American West*. But glancing over from the other end of the bench, a man with skin like white raisins slowly, feebly raised a hand and pinched his bulbous nose between two frail fingers and spoke.

"It *shtinks*," he said.

"What does?" I replied, sniffing my underarms, for it was a hot summer day.

"Dat book," he replied.

"You've read it?"

"Nah," he said. "I lived it."

"Pardon?"

He didn't seem to have heard. "Unless you vas dere, you don't know what really happened about anyting."

I studied him suspiciously. "You were there? The American West?"

"Boychick," he replied, "witout me dere would not be an American West, at least not like we know it."

This man, whose name I would discover was Jack Wiener—he pronounced it "whiner"—proceeded to tell me one of the most startling stories I've ever heard. Luckily, when I smelled myself, I happened to activate "Record" on the portable music player in my pocket, so I am able to report the memoir exactly as it was told to me:

I was born in Nebraska in a loch cabin. It really was just a hole in the ground with a door you pulled down on top of you. It was not very sunny, but it did very well during tornados. My parents were what we now refer to as "pioneers" but at the time were called "shmucks." They left Baltimore in a buggy to find a land which they heard was flowing with milk and money. Which was very true, if you were a gentile with cows and bulls. We were Jews with *bubkes* so we ended up in the woods outside Pawnee City, which was built for the Pawnee—no Jews allowed, which tells you how high we rated.

One morning, when I was still but an infant, my mother went with me to the river to wash our cloth. That is the singular of clothes, right? Because my father and mother and I had just one shmatta each, the same ones we had in Baltimore. Well, mother wasn't watching my basket very closely—at least, I hope that was the case—and it was swept down the river with me in it, like Moses in Egypt. And also like the great patriarch, I was found by a ruler's daughter—in this case, the infertile Dead Beaver, daughter of the Pawnee Chief named Line Stops Here. I was regarded as a gift of the fish spirit—the carp, for they said I complained from the moment they drew me fourth. And I do mean "fourth," for they waited until after they had pulled out the three fish nets before they bothered saving me.

I was named Basket Child, though I may have misheard; it could have been a reference to my unknown parentage. I was raised as an Indian, which wasn't so bad because they dovened like Jews. With my nose and a good tan, I could pass.

When I was seven, I borrowed an outfit from my older brother who was also adopted and of Chinese heritage. His name was Found Ling. We went with several of the Indians to Fort Sidney Blumenthal to trade blankets and other trinkets with the soldiers. I did such a good job that Commander Jacob Wiener came over and had a little talk with me. Seems my breechcloth was a little large, and he noticed that I was not an Indian but a Hebrew. He adopted me as his very own, named me Jack, and I was indoctrinated into the ways of my people.

In other words, I kept selling, but for him.

Commander Wiener had a little side business. He sold easy detail to soldiers who were willing to pay. Now, that wasn't legal, so he wanted me to collect the cash.

Of course, he never counted on two things. One, I didn't want to stay at the fort. And two, he gave me the wherewithal to get away. Over the next two years I skimmed as much money as I could. Finally, with a hundred dollars of easy detail money in my pocket, I borrowed a horse, rode through the gate, and never looked back. However, there was one goal Commander Wiener had given me: I wanted to be Bar Mitzvahed, for it seemed like a good way to make a great deal of money for very little work.

That led me to seek something called *haftorah*, which he mentioned as being necessary for the ceremony. Traveling throughout the Midwest, I found a merchant who was willing to get a pair of scissors and sell me a half-Torah, but I didn't see how that would help. Finally, I met a *chazen* who was eating tomatoes as they dripped from both his forehead and from the stocks which held him.

"I guess maybe I shouldn't have got off the stage at a place called Brown Shirt," he lamented.

I freed the cantor, and he sat in back of me as we rode from town. That was a good place for him to be, since he was able to catch thrown lettuce to go with the tomatoes.

I asked him where he was going, and he said he was looking for a legendary place known as the Seven Cities of Goldberg.

"It is said to have been founded by Russian Jews who took the lantsman bridge to Alaska a thousand years ago," he told me.

"It is said by whom?" I asked him.

"My *mechutunim* back in New Jersey."

"I see. Do you get along with your in-laws?"

"Not so much," he admitted. "They wanted their daughter to marry a lawyer. I figured if I found the Seven Cities they would like me better."

Well, we moved here and there keeping an eye open for this Seven Cities of Goldberg. In the meantime, the *chazen* and I struck up a friendship. In exchange for letting him travel with me, I got lessons in *haftorah*. This bein' a very different time and all, no one thought much of a grown man—and a clergyman at that—travellin' with a boy who was not his kin.

What I did to earn money during this time was to buy blankets and fans from my former Indian tribe and then sell them to settlers. I did very well with these Pawnee shops. I made it possible for thousands of pioneers to make it across the hot plains and freezing mountains. Otherwise, like I said, the West would never have been settled—or shtetled, as the *chazen* described the mud huts and log cabins.

One day we made an extended stop for Simchat Topeka. This holiday was the *chazen*'s own idea for spreading good will and begging alms, though dancing with a Torah scroll proved less of a draw than the guy who juggled hot branding irons. I know because I went to see him myself. It was during this sit-down that I was Bar Mitzvahed. And let me tell you, was I upset to learn from the *chazen* that riches did not come automatically from some Today I Am A Man organization, but from guests at a "reception." That was a real disappointment. I would've written to Commander Wiener to complain but, ironically, I did not own a fountain pen.

Tired of selling Pawnee *tchatchkes*, I made a momentous decision. The *chazen* was returning East, and I decided to go with him. I wanted to see the cities, the rivers rich with gefilte fish, and, most importantly, Jewish women. I had heard of these people, but as yet had never actually seen one other than the mother who set me adrift. Surely all Jewish women could not be so dismissive of their men.

We set out on horseback across the alkalai flats with its famous geyser, then made our way east by rail. My companion stopped to study the salts; he seemed in no hurry to reach our destination, a place named Atlantic City. I understood why when I met the *meshpuchah*. My education in the ways of my people was quick and thorough. I met a rebbe, a man who dressed and sounded and harangued like a medicine man but without the curative powers. I met a litvak, who was like an Arapaho or Apache who no one trusted even though he was one of you. And I met a *macher*, who was just like the Indian agents: He knew many people, but it didn't do you any good.

And, yes, I met Jewish women. There was the *yenta*, who was like a squaw who had consumed loco weed.

I met a *ballabosteh*, who reminded me of a buffalo in a house dress. There was the cute little *maideleh* who wanted to be a ballet dancer until she became a *maidel*, at which point she suddenly wanted to be the wife of a doctor or a lawyer. These women made me so crazy that my stomach hurt, which made me wish I had an old Pawnee remedy.

"What remedy?" the *chazen* asked, only slightly less distressed to be home again.

"The alkalai salts and water," I told him.

"Bubee, you're in luck. I took some of those salts as a souvenir," he informed me, as he grabbed a handful from his kit. He reached for a blue bottle filled with sparkling water, then filled a glass and dropped in the salts. I downed it in a single draught.

The alkalai-seltzer made me feel better almost at once, which gave me an idea. I suggested that we go back to the flats, get trunkfuls of the salts, and sell them to people with upset stomachs.

"Yes," said the *chazen*. "We can call it *Tsuris* Powder."

We didn't call it that, as you probably figured out, but the *chazen* and I made so much money that he was able to hire maids to keep his wife from complaining to him, and I was able to buy a nice house and some fountain pens.

Then Jack Wiener fell silent, and I sat in silence for a long, long moment as I considered his story.

"I assume you also sold your interest in Tsuris Powder, and the new owner renamed it," I said at last.

"Actually, no," he sighed. "Ve just got tired of shlepping back and forth to the flats and stopped. Someone else took our idea and made the real killing."

"What about your house in Atlantic City?"

"The Jew and the Indian in me vas conflicted," he said. "The Jew wanted to sell it, the Indian said, 'Hold on! This can be a casino one day!'"

"And—?"

"Unfortunately, just like in de Vest, the Indian lost. I did okay, though. I invested what I made. I'm comfortable."

The sun was setting and it was time for me to go. I tucked the book under my arm and told Mr. Wiener that I was very happy to have met him.

"I do have one more question," I said. "What happened to the *chazen*? Did he continue singing?"

"Yes. He moved to de Holy Land."

"Israel?"

"Salt Lake City," Wiener replied. "He used his money to start a choir. Dat idea got stolen too."

Maybe Wiener and the *chazen* didn't exactly shape the saga of the Westward expansion, but they were mensches who contributed to the American oral tradition, both singing and *grepsing*.

"One more thing," I said as he shuffled off. "Where did you acquire that Jewish accent?"

The short fellow shrugged his bony shoulders. "I'm an old Jewish man. Like an enlarged prostate, it just heppens."

"Why didn't you acquire an Indian accent, too?"

"How?" he replied.

"Because you lived with them."

"Old Jewish men tell old jokes, too," he smiled and winked as he walked away.

A Fistful of Dreidels

The tall man leaned against the side of the cart, drawing slowly on a slender cigar. The Arizona sun beat mercilessly on bronzed skin that had long ago ceased to feel its impact. The horses hitched to the cart didn't mind it either, having recently drunk their fill at a trough across the street.

Two cooks, cleaning pans in that trough, watched the man as he waited for a door behind him to open.

"They say he rolls them himself," one man whispered to his coworker.

"Everyone does, Lee!" the other replied through a chaw.

Lee looked at him curiously. "I mean, what he came to pick up and deliver to Yuma, Eli."

"Huh?"

"Dreidels."

"You mean that sissy Jew toy?" laughed the other.

"Shhh!" the first man warned. "He might hear you!"

"So?"

"Look at his hips."

Eli regarded the man. Holstered around his narrow waist were a pair of six-shooters. The cook's eyes narrowed. "Lee, is that a cameo on his gun butts?"

"Yup," said the first. "Those are Pearl-handled revolvers. Pearl is his mother."

Eli started to guffaw, but Lee slapped a wet palm on his mouth.

"Don't! A man once laughed at her picture at the saloon," Lee cautioned. "The last thing the fella saw was her puss up close before his brains took a ride out the back of his head."

The men fell silent as woodworker Matt Tell emerged from his shop.

"I've got three crates ready to go, Mr. Josephs," said the craftsman. "The usual?"

"The usual," Josephs replied. He ground out his smoke then stepped into the dark shop, his spurs ringing on the hardwood floor. He lifted the top from one of the three crates, pulled aside the packing straw, dug a strong hand deep, and selected a wooden dreidel at random. He studied the point.

"Top tip, tip top," the woodworker remarked.

Just then, the floorboards creaked above them. Josephs looked up, his hand on his gun butt.

"It's my own dear mama," Tell said anxiously, nodding toward the likenesses of Pearl. "She's a late sleeper."

Josephs relaxed and knelt. Glancing at a grandfather clock in the corner, he gave the dreidel a spin. He bent close, first turning an ear toward the toy. It hummed softly with no variations in pitch. Then he sat back on his heels and watched it turn. There was no wobble. Finally, he flicked the toy with a fingertip. The dreidel scooted a short distance but continued spinning.

He waited until it fell then squinted at the clock. "A minute and eight seconds," Josephs said. "Not bad."

"Kicks some *tuckas*, eh?"

"It's *tuchas*," Josephs said firmly but uncritically as he returned the dreidel to the crate. He was used to hearing foreign languages mispronounced in the West, from the Mojave Desert to the Gila River. "They're better than the ones we used to sell. No one liked waiting until they were dry and ready."

"Boy howdy, you really have a sense of Yuma," Tell said.

Josephs paid cash then carried the crates to his cart. He would take them to Mack Kay Bee Toys in the aforesaid Arizona city. Mack only sold the finest handcrafted items and he liked to have an ample supply of dreidels for Hanukkah when Jews from Chicago arrived for their winter time shares.

Josephs climbed into the seat and urged the twin horses on their way. The cooks nodded respectfully as he passed.

"*Shalom aleikem!*" one cried after him.

"It's *aleichem*," Josephs muttered, puffing smoke from a freshly lit cigar.

However, the cooks weren't the only ones who noted Josephs' departure. From a window above the woodworker's shop, Ramón Yoyo looked down on the dreidel delivery man.

"*Vamos!*" he said to his brother Esteban. "It is time we put our stamp on the holiday season."

"*Bueno!* I've always wanted our very own Christmas seal," cheered Esteban.

Ramón just stared at his brother who stood behind him playing with their own creation, a wooden spool, which was bisected by a cord. There was a slipknot around the man's finger, and he was flipping the toy down and up, down and up.

"*No, idiota!*" Ramón said. "We will stop Josephs and go to Mack Kay Bee ourselves. Soon, our toy will be the favored gift of the holiday season."

"But, *mi hermano*, we still do not have a name for it."

"I've been thinking about that," answered Ramón. "We will call it a yo-yo after our family name. However, since we also want to sell to the Jews, we will tell them it is an 'oy-oy.'"

The grizzled Esteban didn't get it but still smiled hideously, the result of many flubbed Around-the-Worlds having knocked out his teeth and jarred his wits.

The men went to a back room where an elderly woman—it was not Mrs. Tell but their own fearsome madre Consuelo—was supervising a team of Chinese workers. The former railworkers were using chopsticks to tie strings to a thick rod between the joined discs the woodworker had carved.

"How are they coming?" Ramón asked.

In response, she picked up one of the toys and segued quickly from a Reverse Loop the Loop to an Over the Shoulder to a Fast Sleeper.

"*Excelente!*" Ramón declared.

"I love how you work a yo-yo, ma," chimed Esteban.

"This is *nada!*" she insisted. "Soon the world will be on a string. Our string!"

"We will make that happen," Ramón assured her, kissing the back of her sainted hand. Then, with his brother in tow—literally, for the string of his plaything had become tangled around Ramón's foot—he raced down the stairs to the back door where their horses and a gang of thugs were waiting along with their Japanese wrangler.

"*Amigos!*" Ramón announced to the half-dozen men. "At long last we men of Spanish descent will get to celebrate our heritage. Let's go persecute a Jew!"

With a rousing cheer the men set off toward the mountain pass where they would get ahead of Josephs and ambush him.

However, Josephs had been transporting Judaica for years. He was aware of the so-called Circumcision Trail and always took precautions before reaching the cut-off. In addition to the Pearl-handled firearms, he kept a loaded Henry rifle on the seat beside him. It was lubricated with pastrami grease, so it would be extra repeating. He also carried additional cartridges hidden on his person, *tefillin* full of lead.

And there was one thing more, something he had picked

up at a trade show years before. This he kept in a small walnut box between himself and the rifle.

Josephs rode until just before sundown, then made camp east of the pass. Anyone looking to head him off would have to wait until morning when the sun would be at his back. Sure enough, the following day, no sooner had he lit a fresh cigar and set off, than the Yoyo Gang rode down the foothills and lined up in front of him.

"Hey, Judio! Don't be afraid!" Esteban sang out.

"Just get down from the cart," said Ramón, raising a hand to shield his eyes from the sun. "We want to take your cargo for a spin!"

Josephs didn't know who these men were or what they wanted, but it didn't matter. They didn't look like paying customers. The lone traveler flipped open the lid of the box beside him At once, eight guns were trained on him. Josephs removed the contents and raised the object slowly, showing it to the gang.

The would-be dreideljackers started to laugh.

"What's that, a little Jew pitchfork?" Esteban chortled.

Josephs said, "It's a menorah, you *shmuck*."

"What's a menorah?" asked Ramón

"What's a 'shmuck'?" asked Esteban, cocking his revolver.

"A shmuck is the singular of *shmeckel*, which is what you fellas are," Josephs replied. "And a menorah is a receptacle for holiday lights."

"Jew candles?" Esteban said, still laughing.

"That's right," Josephs replied. "Only this one is special."

"How so?" Ramón asked warily.

Josephs grinned around his cigar as he angled the menorah toward the men. "It was manufactured by Colt."

At once, eight candlestick holders spit lead. As an added benefit, the flash from the gunpowder ignited a small wick of the shamah in the center. While the men yelped and winced from pain, Josephs used the flame to reignite his cigar. He blew out the wick, set the candelabrum back in its box, then drew his Pearl-handled revolvers and walked over to the line of wounded attackers. Each had been shot in the gun hand by the strategically spaced candle-holders.

"What did you think of my 'fire' arm?" Josephs asked as he retrieved their fallen guns.

"*Madre de Dios*, that is some weapon," Ramón commented, gripping his bloody fingers.

"You hurt my yoyo hand!" Esteban cried.

"*Tahkeh*, who else's?"

"No, I mean you hurt my yo-yo hand!"

Josephs didn't bother to reply.

"What are you going to do with us now?" asked Ramón.

"He's going to make us wander in the desert like Hebrew slaves with nothing but Jew bread to parch our mouths," Esteban went on.

"It's matzo, you moron," Josephs said.

A gang member looked at the revolvers and shuddered. "He's gonna chew us down!"

Josephs glared at the man. "Did you say 'Jew'?"

"No, I said 'chew,' I swear it!"

"*Silencio!*" Ramón ordered. He looked at Josephs. "Señor, we did not want to rob you. We don't even like robbing! Our mother makes us do it."

"Is this true?" Josephs asked the others.

They all nodded.

"Well, I can understand that kind of pressure from one's mother," Josephs said. "*A sof,* we're going to ride to the creek, so you can wash and bandage your hands. Then you're coming with me."

"What for?" a gang member demanded.

"You'll find out. Either that," he aimed his guns at the man's horse, "or you can stay out here and bleed to death."

"You would allow us to perish?" asked the Japanese, who had come with his employer.

"*Si,*" answered Ramón, taking the measure of the man. "He would let us die, die, *Ainu.*"

The men agreed to their captor's terms and by sunset they had reached Mack Kay Bee's store. When Josephs had finished his transaction he bought a dreidel for himself then took the men to a saloon at the end of Main Street. It was a Chinese establishment.

"Gentlemen, as it happens, you all jumped the gun," Josephs told them. "See, this was my last trip. I finally saved enough to buy this place. Now, I've got a manager, but I need men to help run it."

And that was how the Wongbranch Saloon became The

Gelt 'n' Horseshoe, the first dreidel gaming parlor in the West. The Yoyos and their gang stayed in Yuma and worked hard and well, not because it was profitable for them or because it was in their natures to do so.

They worked because they were motivated by the manager.

You see, Josephs had a mother, too.

3:10 to Boca

As the train pulled from Pennsylvania Station, New York, on its way to Boca Raton, Florida, Ben Vaigets staggered into the dining car. He had been unable to find a carriage and had run all the way from his apartment on the East Side. There had been no time to buy anything to go, leaving the young attorney hungry and in no mood for the *ahzes punim* porter who greeted him with:

"We're not open yet, sir."

"Look," Vaigets said, showing his ticket. "I'm on my way to visit my parents. I'm going there to tell them in person that I broke it off with my fiancée. That's bad enough without having to do sit here with an empty stomach. All I want is a plain bagel. I'm sure you can rustle that up."

"Sir," the porter insisted, "if I serve you, I have to serve everyone." He pointed to a line of people who had already begun collecting outside the door.

"*Gevald*," moaned Vaigets. "Now I won't even be first!"

The passenger reached into his pocket and removed his

Jewish bankroll. He pulled the ten from atop the wad of singles and forced it into the porter's hand.

"I'm sorry, sir, I can't accept this."

"Believe me, it hurts me worse to offer it," Vaigets said. "But I'm dying here."

Vaigets' eyes drifted to the line of waiting patrons. They were like an angry rattlesnake—which he had never actually seen, except on Discovery HD. The man in front was literally watching him with wide eyes and a slithering tongue.

"No, sir," the porter said, pushing the man's hand away.

His temper as high as his blood sugar was low, the lawyer reached past the porter, rushed to the counter, and grabbed an onion bagel wrapped in wax paper. When the passengers outside saw what he was doing, something snapped: the lock on the door. The snakelike mob ran in, laptops tucked safely under their arms like footballs, and threw themselves at Vaigets.

"*Shteyner af zayne beyner!*" the attorney cried as, reaching for the condiments, he pelted them with bottles of cream and sugar cubes. The indignant passengers slipped and skidded on the suddenly slickened floor, ending in a wounded heap in the aisle. Making for the opposite door, Vaigets lost himself in the first-class cabin.

"There's nowhere to go!" cried the man who had been the eyes and tongue of the snake. "This is a train!"

"We'll get you!" the porter yelled from beneath a pile of commuting humanity. "You have a coach ticket!"

Uninjured in the confrontation was Dan Fonfer, a strapping young plumber who was leaving the Bronx to try and make more money in the leaking beachfronts of Florida. Slipping away during the confusion, he spotted Vaigets as the man exited the train in Newark and immediately doubled back toward the sleeper cabins. Following him, Fonfer sniffed. Year of unclogging stuffed drains had left him with a nose for food and hair. The scent of the onion bagel was as familiar to him as Drano.

Corralling a conductor, Fonfer pointed out the Presidential Suite.

"The man you want is in there," Fonfer said.

The crowd from the dining car was back on their feet and hunting their prey. Gray Putgerfield, who was in fact a semiconductor, entered the room and found Vaigets sitting on the open bed, eating the onion bagel.

"Let me see your ticket!" Putgerfield challenged, wanting to keep this legal. He whipped out his puncher and twirled it on his index finger.

His lips coated with what looked like cream cheese, Vaigets simply sat there and smiled.

Unfortunately for the group, the cabin had been rented by Charlie Pritzeh, a *faigeleh* who just then emerged from the very nice combination lavatory-shower. The young man was naked, wet, and wearing a skimpy towel. He glared angrily at the intruders.

"I've already had my ticket punched," he said.

"Sir," said Putgerfield, tipping his hat respectfully, "we're here for the other party."

"There's another party?" Pritzeh said. "Do tell!"

"I mean we're here for this individual," the semi-conductor replied, his face reddening.

"I'll be happy to share," Pritzeh said provocatively.

It was a Yiddish standoff: how much aggravation is money worth?

Not this much, it seemed.

With grumbles of displeasure, the group left. Only the porter and plumber Fonfer remained.

"The others may have gone," the porter told Vaigets, "but I'm not leaving until you give me two bits for the food plus another four bits for the cream and sugar you busted up."

"That will be my treat," Pritzeh said, reaching for his handbag.

When accounts had been settled, the porter left and Pritzeh put his bag back on the shelf.

"Disbursed, dispersed, and depursed," he smiled.

Now only Fonfer remained. He regarded Vaigets coldly.

"Is this really what you want?" Fonfer asked. "To be a male *kurveh*, selling your body?"

The lawyer shrugged. "If I show up with him, the news about my fiancée won't seem so bad."

Fonfer shook his head. "This is why I'm a simple plumber and not a lawyer."

Pritzeh gestured toward the shower. "Care to check some pipe, my hunky *grubber yung*?"

"Gay *avek*," Fonfer said with ironic appropriateness as he turned, shaking his head. "I'm going back to the Bronx and I'll never complain about being a poor wrencher again."